COUNTRY KITCHEN
Cookbook

Introduction

When I have a food craving, it's rarely for something delicate with a subtle flavor. Nope!—I want big, bold, spicy, cheesy, meaty, melt-in-my-mouth goodness. And a piece of pie or cake at the end!

There's nothing more comforting than a big country meal. It fills you up and reminds you of old-fashioned meals your mom used to serve (or you wish she used to serve): Southern classics like Pork Ribs with Honey BBQ Sauce and Cowboy Beans, bubbly baked dishes like Spicy Chicken Macaroni and Tater Tot Casserole, party-pleasers like Classic Pimento Cheese and Barbecue Meatball Minis, creative spins on old favorites like Red Velvet Pancakes and Apple Upside-Down Cake, and of course, plenty of country desserts like Cinnamon-Apple Crumble, Mississippi Mud Cake, Farm-Stand Whoopie Pies, and much more.

There's nothing more delicious than country cooking, and there's also nothing more American than a big country meal.

Since my mother's mother was from the South and my dad's was from the Midwest, many of the recipes in this book come from those two regions. But I couldn't make a country cooking book without including lots of recipes from the capital of country cooking, Louisiana. For those recipes and ones from the country regions of New England, the Southwest, and more, I relied on friends and my own life-long experimentation with casseroles, party hors d'oeuvres, and supermarket foods (I could write a whole book on my fondness for Mexican four-cheese blend!).

Most of the recipes inside are easy to make and inexpensive (check out the Carolina Pulled Pork Sandwiches if you need to feed a big crowd for less than $20), while a few "above and beyond" recipes are included for when you're in a mood to cook (make the Caramel-Apple French Toast on someone's birthday and they're sure to feel special). Most are easily adaptable to you and your family's tastes—use whatever herbs you have handy, and throw what beans or veggies were on sale into dishes like the Down-Home Chili and Easy Gumbo. Add some hot sauce if that's your thing! Making it how you want it is a country tradition.

Most of all, enjoy the wonderful smells wafting through your home, and the family they're sure to attract to your kitchen. Because country cooking isn't as delicious without a crowd.

Homestyle Breakfasts

SUNDAY CASSEROLE

This casserole is perfect for feeding a hungry family just home from church. Make it the night before and store it in the refrigerator, then stick it in the oven as soon as you come home for a hot brunch worth gathering around the table for.

Ingredients

5 slices bacon
1 medium onion, chopped
1 large tomato, cored and chopped
8 large eggs, beaten
1½ cups shredded cheddar
 cheese, divided
½ teaspoon paprika
1 teaspoon salt
¾ teaspoon black pepper
2 cups frozen shredded hash-
 brown potatoes, thawed

Directions

1. Preheat oven to 375°F.

2. Place bacon in medium skillet, then heat to medium-low. Cook, flipping once, until cooked through and edges start to curl, about 8–12 minutes. Remove bacon to paper towels to drain. When cool, crumble into pieces.

3. Drain all but 1 tablespoon of fat from skillet. Then, add onion.

Increase heat to medium-high and cook, stirring occasionally, until onion is tender, about 3 minutes.

4. In medium bowl, combine onion, tomato, eggs, half of cheese, paprika, salt, and pepper.

5. Press shredded hash browns into bottom of greased 13x9-inch casserole dish. Top with egg mixture, bacon, and remaining cheese.

6. Bake, covered, for 30 minutes, then uncover and bake until cheese on top just starts to brown, about 10–15 minutes more.

Makes 8 servings.

HOME-FRIED SAUSAGE CASSEROLE

Home fries form the base of this cheesy casserole that's my favorite way to dress up frozen breakfast sausage.

Ingredients
2 cups frozen home-fried or diced hash-brown potatoes
1 (7- or 8-ounce) package frozen breakfast sausage links
1 tablespoon unsalted butter
1 medium yellow onion, chopped
2 large eggs, beaten
1½ cups shredded cheddar cheese
¼ teaspoon garlic powder
¼ teaspoon dried thyme
½ teaspoon paprika

Directions
1. Preheat oven to 400°F.

2. Prepare potatoes and breakfast sausage as package directs. Cut breakfast links into bite-sized slices.

3. In small skillet over medium-high heat, heat butter until melted. Then add onion and cook, stirring occasionally, until soft, about 3–5 minutes.

4. In large bowl, combine onion, potatoes, sausage, eggs, cheese, garlic powder, and thyme. Fold together with wooden spoon to combine, then pour into lightly greased 13x19-inch casserole dish. Sprinkle with paprika.

5. Cover with aluminum foil and bake until cheese is just melted, about 20–25 minutes. Remove foil and bake until cheese starts to turn golden around the edges of the casserole dish, about 5–10 minutes more.

Makes 8 servings.

FULL BELLIES BREAKFAST SKILLET

Nothing says "breakfast is served!" like this platter of goodness. With bacon, eggs, and potatoes, it's everything you want in a breakfast, all in one place.

Ingredients
6 slices bacon
½ medium onion, chopped
3 medium potatoes, boiled and cubed, or 2 cups frozen home-fried or diced hash-brown potatoes, thawed
½ teaspoon salt
½ teaspoon black pepper
¾ cup shredded cheddar cheese
4 large eggs
1 tablespoon chopped fresh cilantro or parsley, for garnish

Directions
1. Preheat oven to 350°F.

2. Place bacon in medium oven-safe skillet, then heat to medium-low. Cook, flipping once, until cooked through and edges start to curl, about 8–12 minutes. Remove bacon to paper towels to drain. Drain all but 2 tablespoons of fat from skillet. Then, add onion and potatoes.

3. Increase heat to medium-high and cook, stirring occasionally, until onion is tender and potatoes start to brown, about 5 minutes. Drain any excess bacon fat.

4. Crumble bacon and sprinkle over potatoes. Sprinkle with salt, pepper, and cheese. Remove from heat. Make 4 indentations in potato mixture. Break 1 egg into each indentation.

5. Bake for 12 to 14 minutes or until eggs are set. Garnish with cilantro or parsley.

Makes 4 servings.

SOUPED-UP POTATO PANCAKE

Potatoes might be just a side dish when paired with a meaty dinner, but in this breakfast dish, they're the star. Sliced thin and layered with egg, they're delicate, delicious, and designed so that you can't eat just one slice.

Ingredients
2 pounds small red potatoes
1 large red bell pepper, finely chopped
½ teaspoon garlic powder or 2 garlic cloves, minced
1½ teaspoons salt
½ teaspoon black pepper
1½ cups grated Parmesan cheese, divided
12 large eggs
1 cup half and half

Directions
1. Preheat the oven to 375°F.

2. Slice potatoes 1/8-inch thick using a mandoline, or slice as thinly as possible with a knife.

3. Spread half of potatoes in bottom of lightly greased 9-inch round baking pan. Mix together bell pepper, garlic, salt, pepper, and ½ cup Parmesan cheese. Spread this mixture over the potatoes.

4. Whisk together eggs, then whisk in half and half and ½ cup Parmesan cheese. Pour about half of egg mixture over the potatoes.

5. Lay remaining potatoes on top in overlapping rows. Pour remaining egg mixture over potatoes, and top with remaining ½ cup Parmesan cheese.

6. Bake until potatoes are fork-tender and top is bubbling and brown, about 1 hour and 15 minutes.

Makes 6–8 servings.

COUNTRY
KITCHEN
Cookbook

Jennifer Boudinot

CHARTWELL
BOOKS

Inspiring | Educating | Creating | Entertaining

Brimming with creative inspiration, how-to projects, and useful information to enrich your everyday life, Quarto Knows is a favorite destination for those pursuing their interests and passions. Visit our site and dig deeper with our books into your area of interest: Quarto Creates, Quarto Cooks, Quarto Homes, Quarto Lives, Quarto Drives, Quarto Explores, Quarto Gifts, or Quarto Kids.

MIX
Paper from
responsible sources
FSC® C016973

Contents

FANCY OVEN EGGS

This oven-baked omelet (or "frittata") is perfect for using up leftover ham and has become an after-Easter staple in my home. If you don't have ham on hand, purchase some at the deli or even sub in some bacon.

Ingredients

8 large eggs
¾ cup 2% milk
1½ cups shredded Mexican four-
　cheese blend
¼ pound cooked ham, chopped
2 medium tomatoes, cut into ½-
　inch thick slices
¾ teaspoon salt
½ teaspoon black pepper
¼ teaspoon dried thyme
⅛ teaspoon dried oregano

Directions

1. Preheat oven to 400°F.

2. Whisk eggs and milk until well combined, then stir in cheese and ham.

3. Arrange tomato slices in overlapping layers in lightly greased oven-safe skillet or greased 9-inch round baking pan. Pour egg mixture on top.

4. Bake for 30–40 minutes until

golden. Cool for 5 minutes and then flip onto platter.

Makes 4 servings.

BACON & TOMATO MUFFINS

Muffins are perfect for an easy breakfast, brunch or light lunch. Make them in advance, then store them overnight or freeze them for a longer period. Reheat them when required.

Ingredients:

1 cup all-purpose flour
1 cup cornmeal
 or polenta
2 tablespoons baking powder
2 eggs, beaten
4 tablespoons butter, melted and
 slightly cooled
1 cup milk
½ canned tomtoes, finely chopped
 and drained.
8 slices of bacon, lightly broiled
 and chopped
Ground black pepper
4 tbsp Parmesan cheese, grated

Directions

1. Mix the flour, cornmeal and baking powder together. Beat in the eggs, butter, and milk, and when well mixed, stir in the tomatoes, bacon and a little pepper. Leave to stand for 10 minutes.

2. Preheat the oven to 375°F.

3. Spoon the mixture into 8 lightly greased deep muffin cups and sprinkle on the cheese. Bake for 10–12 minutes until well risen and golden.

4. Serve warm with butter or a bowl of crème fraîche or fromage frais.

Makes 8 servings.

APPLE AND CINNAMON MUFFINS

These quick and simple-to-make muffins are delicious for breakfast or brunch. If you make them the day before, don't refrigerate them but store them in an airtight container, returning them to a hot oven for 5 minutes before serving.

Ingredients
2 cups all-purpose flour
½ teaspoon salt
1 teaspoon ground cinnamon
3 tablespoons superfine sugar
2 eggs, beaten
Scant cup milk
4 tablespoons butter, melted
1 large sweet apple, skinned, cored and diced
4 tablespoons raisins

Directions
1. Preheat the oven to 375°F. Lightly grease a 12-muffin pan, or use muffin cups and place them on cookie sheets ready for filling.

2. Sift the flour, salt and cinnamon into a bowl and add the sugar. Beat the eggs, milk and melted butter together, then stir into the dry ingredients. Add the diced apple and raisins and stir in lightly.

3. Divide the mixture up and bake for 30 minutes or until well risen and just firm to the touch. Serve warm with melted butter or cold with ice cream or crème fraîche.

Makes 10–12 servings.

BANANA & CHOCOLATE BREAD

A great treat, this bread becomes even moister when kept for a day or two, though this is easier said than done in the face of such temptation.

Ingredients
¾ cup butter or margarine
Scant cup light brown sugar
Few drops of vanilla extract
1 tablespoon lemon juice
3 bananas, mashed
3 eggs, beaten

2 cups all-purpose flour, sifted
1 teaspoon baking powder
⅓ cup chocolate chips

Directions
1. Cream the butter and sugar together until the mixture is light and fluffy. Combine the vanilla extract with the lemon juice and bananas, then blend them into the butter and sugar mixture. Preheat oven to 325°F.

2. Gradually fold in the beaten eggs, alternating them with the flour mixed with the baking powder, then add chocolate chips. When blended, spoon into a greased 2-lb loaf pan or 8-inch lined cake pan.

3. Bake in a loaf pan for about 1 hour or until firm to the touch. Cool in the pan before turning out.

Serves 6–8 servings.

CRANBERRY-ORANGE MONKEY BREAD

Monkey bread for breakfast is a holiday tradition at my house. Kids love anything they can eat with their hands, and everyone reaching in to grab pieces of sweet, sticky bread always seems like a festive way for the whole family (kids and adults alike) to start the day.

Ingredients
½ cup granulated sugar
1 teaspoon cinnamon
¼ teaspoon nutmeg
¾ teaspoon orange zest

2 (16.3-ounce) cans refrigerated flaky biscuit dough
½ cup dried cranberries
1 cup light brown sugar
¾ cup unsalted butter, melted

Directions
1. Heat oven to 350°F. Lightly grease Bundt pan with shortening or cooking spray.

2. In shallow bowl, mix together granulated sugar, cinnamon, nutmeg, and orange zest.

3. Separate dough into 16 biscuits; cut each into quarters. Dredge biscuit quarters in sugar mixture to coat. Arrange in pan, adding cranberries in between biscuit pieces.

4. In small bowl, mix brown sugar and butter; pour over biscuit pieces.

5. Bake 28–32 minutes, or until golden brown and no longer doughy in center. Cool in pan 10 minutes. Turn upside down onto serving plate; pull apart to serve. Serve warm.

Makes 6–8 servings.

CHOCOLATE CHIP PANCAKES

When I was growing up, the only thing that made my mom's pancakes during Saturday morning cartoons any better is when she threw some leftover chocolate chips in there as a surprise. If you're cooking for a crowd and not just a hungry kid who likes her pancakes one-by-one, set your oven on its lowest setting and place finished pancakes in a casserole dish inside to keep them warm.

Ingredients
1 cup all-purpose flour
1 tablespoon sugar
2 teaspoons baking powder
Pinch of salt
1 large egg
1 cup 2% milk
2 tablespoons vegetable oil
1 cup chocolate chips

Directions
1. In medium bowl, combine flour, sugar, baking powder, and salt.

2. In separate medium bowl, add egg, milk, and vegetable oil and whisk to combine well.

3. Make an indentation in the middle of flour mixture, then pour in egg mixture and mix until incorporated and lumps just start to disappear. Fold in chocolate chips.

4. Heat lightly greased 12-inch skillet over medium heat. Then pour about ¼ cup batter onto skillet. Flip when bubbles in batter start to pop, about 2 minutes. Cook on other side until both sides are golden brown, about 2 minutes more. Serve with butter and maple syrup.

Makes 4–5 servings.

RED VELVET PANCAKES WITH CREAM CHEESE BUTTER

I might be giving away a secret when I tell you that red velvet cake – a Southern specialty – is just cocoa powder and red food coloring. Add these ingredients to pancakes instead and you have a chocolaty breakfast that's so fun it feels like dessert.

Ingredients
Pancakes
1 cup all-purpose flour
½ cup unsweetened cocoa powder
1 tablespoon granulated sugar
1 teaspoon baking soda
¼ teaspoon salt
1 large egg
½ cup 2% or whole milk
½ cup sour cream
2 tablespoons red liquid food coloring
½ of 1 (1 pint) container fresh raspberries, for garnish

Cream Cheese Butter
½ of 1 (8-ounce) package cream cheese, softened
½ cup unsalted butter, softened
½ teaspoon vanilla extract
1½ cups powdered sugar

Directions
Pancakes
1. In medium bowl, combine flour,

cocoa powder, sugar, baking soda, and salt.

2. In separate medium bowl, add egg, milk, sour cream, and food coloring, and whisk to combine well.

3. Make an indentation in the middle of flour mixture, then pour in egg mixture and mix until red color is incorporated throughout.

4. Heat lightly greased 12-inch skillet over medium heat. Then pour about ¼ cup batter onto skillet. Flip when bubbles in batter start to pop, about 1½ minutes.

Cook on other side until both sides are golden brown, about 1 minute more. Top with cream cheese butter, and raspberries.

Cream Cheese Butter
1. In large bowl, beat cream cheese, butter, and vanilla extract with electric hand mixer on medium until well-blended.

2. While beating at low speed, slowly add powdered sugar, allowing it to incorporate after each addition, until well-blended.

Makes 4–5 servings.

CARAMEL-APPLE FRENCH TOAST

This decadent breakfast is fit for breakfast in bed from the most romantic person in the world . . . I'm still waiting. In the meantime, I can always make it for special brunches or even as a dessert.

Ingredients

Apples
4 apples, peeled, cored, and sliced into thin wedges
1 teaspoon ground cinnamon
¾ cup light brown sugar
¼ teaspoon ground nutmeg
⅛ teaspoon salt

Caramel Syrup
¾ cup buttermilk
1¼ cups granulated sugar
½ cup unsalted butter
2 tablespoons corn syrup
1 teaspoon baking soda
1 teaspoon vanilla extract

French Toast
2 large eggs
½ cup 2% or whole milk
¼ teaspoon vanilla extract
¼ teaspoon ground cinnamon
5 slices French bread, each 1-inch thick
1 tablespoon unsalted butter
Vanilla ice cream, for serving

Directions

Apples
1. Preheat oven to 375°F.

2. Place apples in medium bowl and gently mix all the ingredients together.

3. Put apple mixture in nonstick baking dish; cover and place in oven. Bake for 45 minutes or until soft, stirring at least once every 15 minutes. Cook for another few minutes to thicken sauce.

Caramel Syrup
1. Combine buttermilk, sugar, butter, corn syrup, and baking soda in large pot. Bring ingredients to a boil and reduce heat to reach low simmer.

2. Cook, stirring frequently, 8–9 minutes or until golden brown. Remove from heat and add vanilla. Stir to incorporate foam on top or skim off if desired.

French Toast
1. In shallow bowl, combine eggs, milk, vanilla, and cinnamon; whisk until well-blended.

2. Dip each slice of bread into egg mixture, allowing bread to become completely saturated, about 20–30 seconds per side.

3. In 12-inch skillet, heat butter over medium heat until melted. Add pieces of bread in batches, cooking until golden brown, about 2–3 minutes per side. Top with apples, caramel syrup, and a scoop of ice cream.

Makes 3–5 servings.

OATMEAL & RAISIN COOKIES

These delicious and satisfying cookies are perfect for breakfast on the go.

Ingredients

¾ cup soft butter
¾ cup white sugar
¾ packed cup light
 brown sugar
2 eggs
1 teaspoon vanilla
 extract
1¼ cups all-purpose
 flour
1 teaspoon baking soda
¾ teaspoon ground
 cinnamon
½ teaspoon salt
2¾ cups rolled oats
1 cup raisins

Directions

1. Preheat the oven to 375°F

2. In a large bowl, cream together the butter and white and brown sugars until smooth.

3. Beat in the eggs and vanilla extract until the mixture is fluffy.

4. In another bowl, stir together the flour, baking soda, cinnamon and salt, then gradually beat into the butter mixture. Stir in the oats and raisins. Using a spoon, drop teaspoonfuls of the mixture onto an ungreased cookie sheet, leaving space for the mixture to spread.

5. Bake for 8–10 minutes or until golden brown, then allow to cool slightly before transferring to a wire rack. Cool completely before eating.

Makes 6–8 servings.

FARM-STYLE BISCUITS & GRAVY

Eating gravy at breakfast time is "normal" in the country, and so is storing bacon fat in your refrigerator or freezer. The next time you make bacon, pour the leftover fat into a mug or other ceramic container, cover with plastic wrap or foil, and place it in the freezer. You can use a knife or spoon to measure out enough fat to make recipes like this come to life with the amazing deliciousness only bacon can add.

Ingredients
Biscuits
¾ cup buttermilk
¼ cup heavy cream
2 large eggs
2¼ cups all-purpose or low-
  protein biscuit flour, such as
  White Lily or Adluh
2 teaspoons baking powder
1 teaspoon salt
1 cup chilled unsalted butter, cut
  into ½-inch slices

Gravy
¼ cup bacon grease
¼ cup all-purpose flour
1½ cups 2% milk, warmed, plus
more as needed
¼ teaspoon salt
¼ teaspoon black pepper

Directions
Biscuits
1. Preheat oven to 400°F.

2. In small bowl, whisk together buttermilk, cream, and 1 egg.

3. In large bowl, whisk together flour, baking powder, and salt.

4. Add butter to flour mixture and toss until fully coated. Working quickly and using your fingers, rub butter into flour until butter forms marble-sized pieces. Alternatively, add flour mixture and butter to food processor and pulse 2–3 times to form marble-sized pieces; transfer to large bowl.

5. Add buttermilk mixture to flour mixture and gently stir with a fork until just combined; the dough should look somewhat dry and shaggy. Cover and let rest in refrigerator for 30 minutes.

6. Turn out dough onto lightly floured work surface. Form dough into a rectangle, lightly pressing and folding to bring it together; avoid squeezing or kneading.

7. Fold dough into thirds like a letter. Using rolling pin, roll out dough and repeat folding once more. Roll out dough to about ½-inch thickness. Wrap in plastic and transfer to refrigerator for 10 minutes.

8. Return dough to work surface, and, using a 3-inch-round cookie-cutter and pressing down without twisting, cut out biscuits as closely together as possible. Gather together scraps, pat down, and cut out more biscuits; discard any remaining scraps.

9. Beat remaining egg and use it to brush top of each biscuit.

10. Bake biscuits about 15 minutes or until risen and golden. Let cool slightly, then transfer to wire rack.

Gravy
1. In medium skillet, heat bacon grease over medium-high heat.

2. Add flour and whisk until smooth and bubbly, about 1 minute.

3. Add warm milk slowly and bring to a boil. Reduce heat to low and simmer, stirring, until thickened, about 5 minutes, adding more milk as necessary to control the thickness. Stir in salt and pepper. Serve hot over biscuits.

Makes 6 servings.

HONEY CHICKEN & CHEDDAR-CHEESE WAFFLES

Chicken paired with waffles is a Southern tradition, but the sweet-and-spicy honey these are drizzled with is anything but. Cheddar cheese added into the batter of these from-scratch waffles will make you really happy you bought that waffle maker!

Ingredients
1 cup all-purpose flour
2 tablespoons sugar
1 teaspoon baking powder
¼ teaspoon salt
1 cup 2% milk
2 large eggs
1 cup shredded cheddar cheese
¼ cup unsalted butter, melted
1 cup honey
2 tablespoons ancho chili powder
10–12 pieces fried chicken (see recipe on page 106)

Directions
1. Preheat waffle iron according to manufacturer's instructions.

2. In large bowl, combine flour, sugar, baking powder, and salt; whisk until well-combined.

3. In small bowl, combine milk and eggs; whisk until well-combined.

4. Pour egg mixture over flour mixture, and whisk gently just until lumps start to disappear. Mix in butter. Fold in cheese.

5. Following manufacturer's instructions, cook waffles until deep brown and crisp. (For a standard waffle iron, pour a generous ½ cup batter into center, spreading to within ½ inch of edges, and close; waffle will cook in 2–3 minutes.)

6. Meanwhile, in small bowl, combine honey and chili powder. Whisk until well-combined.

7. Top waffles with chicken and spicy honey.

Makes 6 servings.

Irresistible Snacks & Starters

HOT CRAB DIP

When I was in college, my friend Charles used have the most fabulous parties – because back then, he was the only one who actually made appetizers! This hot crab dip recipe still makes its way into onto my party spread today.

Ingredients
1 tablespoon unsalted butter
1 (8-ounce) package cream cheese, softened
¾ cup mayonnaise
¼ teaspoon garlic powder
1 teaspoon prepared horseradish, drained
1 teaspoon Worcestershire sauce
¼ teaspoon salt
⅛ teaspoon black pepper
½ teaspoon hot sauce (optional)
1 (6-ounce) can fancy lump crabmeat
1 tablespoon slivered almonds
1 tablespoon chopped scallions, for garnish (optional)
Crackers for serving

Directions
1. Preheat oven to 325°F. Butter 2-cup oven-safe dish.

2. In medium bowl, mix together cream cheese, mayonnaise, garlic powder, horseradish, Worcestershire sauce, salt, pepper, and hot sauce, if using, until smooth. Fold in crabmeat and almonds. Transfer mixture to prepared dish.

3. Bake until heated through, about 25 minutes. Serve with crackers. Garnish with scallions if desired.

Makes about 2 cups.

SPINACH-ARTICHOKE DIP

If there's a more delicious way to eat spinach, I haven't tasted it. Hollow out a loaf of sourdough bread to make an impressive serving dish for this classic hors d'oeuvre.

Ingredients

1 (14-ounce) can artichoke hearts, drained and finely chopped
1 (10-ounce) package frozen chopped spinach, thawed and well-drained
¾ cup grated Parmesan cheese
¾ cup mayonnaise
½ cup shredded mozzarella cheese
½ teaspoon garlic powder
½ teaspoon hot sauce
½ teaspoon salt
1 sourdough bread round, for serving (optional)
Crackers, for serving

Directions

1. Heat oven to 350°F.

2. In medium bowl, combine all ingredients. Spoon mixture into lightly greased 9-inch quiche dish or pie plate.

3. Bake 20 minutes or until heated through.

4. Scoop out middle of sourdough bread, if desired, and use to serve dip with remaining sourdough and crackers.

Makes about 4 cups.

CLASSIC PIMENTO CHEESE

You may have come across pimento cheese as an appetizer at a party, but for Southerners, it's a way of life! Spread it on toast, use it to top a burger, even put it in an omelet to give any meal or snack a spicy, cheesy kick.

Ingredients

6 ounces cream cheese

½ cup shredded extra-sharp white cheddar cheese

¾ cup shredded sharp cheddar cheese

1 cup shredded Monterey Jack cheese

1 cup mayonnaise

1 (4-ounce) jar pimientos, drained and chopped

½ teaspoon garlic powder

¾ teaspoon Worcestershire sauce

1 teaspoon hot sauce

¼ teaspoon black pepper

Directions

1. Using electric hand mixer, beat cream cheese until soft.

2. Add remaining ingredients and beat until creamy and combined.

3. Cover and refrigerate for about an hour.

Makes about 3 cups.

EASY CHILI CON QUESO

Chili and cheese are a natural pairing, and in this recipe, they're an easy one, too. The spiciness of the chili is balanced out by the sweet creaminess of — surprise — cream cheese! Everyone will be wondering what your secret is.

Ingredients

1 (8-ounce) package cream cheese, softened
1 (15-ounce) can no-bean chili
½ cup shredded cheddar cheese
½ teaspoon salt
½ teaspoon hot sauce (optional)
Tortilla chips, for serving

Directions

1. In medium saucepan, combine all ingredients and cook over medium heat, stirring constantly, until bubbly, about 5 minutes.

2. Pour into blender and blend until smooth.

3. Serve warm with tortilla chips.

Makes 6–8 appetizer portions.

CREAMY CRAB SOUP

Crab, whether softshell, freshwater or spiny, is a strong favorite in the south, and can be used to produce a deliciously rich soup, while corn is of course a traditional extra which is very popular throughout the whole of America. Most important, though, is to make a good stock first.

Ingredients:
Stock
Shells of 2 crabs (or 1 crab and
 lobster)
1 lb fresh shrimp or crawfish
1 large onion, quartered
1 peeled carrot
2 sticks of celery
Few bay leaves
Few black peppercorns
Water to cover (about 5 cups)
Juice of ½ lemon
1–2 glasses of alcohol-free white
 wine
Parsley stalks
Salt

Soup
4 tablespoons butter or
 sunflower oil
1 large onion, finely chopped
3 cloves of garlic, finely chopped
1 red or yellow pepper, seeded
 and finely chopped
2 sticks of celery, thinly sliced

½ cup flour
3¾ cups good seafood or fish
 stock (Step 1.)
1 lb fresh crabmeat, taken from the
body and claws
 and kept in chunks
¾ cup heavy cream
Salt and pepper
Extra cream to serve

Directions
1. Place the first eight stock ingredients in a very large pan. Bring to a boil and bubble gently for 30–40 minutes or until reduced

by half. Add the lemon juice, wine, the parsley stalks, and salt to taste. Bring back to a boil and simmer for a further 15 minutes. Strain, and check the seasoning again before use.

2. Melt the butter in a large pan and gently cook the onion, garlic, peppers and celery until all have become soft but not browned.

3. Stir in the flour and blend until all the fat is absorbed. Cook for 1–2 minutes to form a thick roux.

4. Gradually add the stock, a little at a time, beating or whisking well to prevent lumps from forming. When all the stock is added, bring to a boil and simmer for 15 minutes.

5. Add the crabmeat chunks and simmer for a further 15 minutes, then blend or sieve the soup to produce a smooth finish.

6. Return to the pan, add the cream and seasonings to taste, and reheat without boiling. Serve topped with an extra swirl of cream.

Makes 4 servings.

HOT PEPPER & BEAN SOUP

With the addition of ground pork or sausage meat, this soup is deeply warming and satisflying. Should a more mellow taste be required, paprika can be substituted for Tabasco sauce.

Ingredients
1 cup of ground pork or sausage
meat
1 cup red or brown beans, or a
mixture of both,
soaked overnight
2 tablespoons butter
1 large onion, finely chopped
2 cloves of garlic, chopped
½ cup corn
1 large leek, well washed and
finely sliced
2 sticks of celery, diced
2 bay leaves
1 ham hock
2 large tomatoes, seeded and
chopped
1 tablespoon tomato purée
Pinch of ground cloves
1 tablespoon Tabasco sauce
Salt
1 tablespoon chopped cilantro or
flat-leaf parsley

Directions
1. Place the soaked, drained beans in a large pan, cover with fresh water, bring to a boil, then simmer for 1–1½ hours or until almost tender. (Do not add salt at this stage or the beans will not soften.)

2. In another large pan, heat the butter and sauté the onion until translucent. Add the garlic, leek and celery and toss them over a high heat for a minute or so.

3. Add the bay leaves and the ham hock, adding sufficient water to cover. Bring to a boil and simmer, covered, for at least one hour, carefully spooning off any scum that rises to the surface. Discard the hock and strain.

4. In a separate pan, fry the ground pork in a little oil until lightly browned.

5. Return the stock to the pan and add the drained beans, ground pork, corn, tomatoes, tomato purée, ground cloves, Tabasco, and salt to taste. Bring to a boil and simmer for a further 30–40 minutes or until the beans are quite tender.

Delicious served with crusty bread.

Makes 4 servings.

CHICKEN NOODLE SOUP

So comforting and nourishing is this classic soup that it has been claimed as a universal panacea, a cure for everything. Thin shreds of chicken can be added to the soup after it has been strained and before serving.

Ingredients

4–5 lb chicken pieces or 1 whole
 chicken
1 small onion, quartered
2 carrots, peeled and chopped
2 sticks of celery, chopped
Salt and black pepper
2 oz of dried linguine
1–2 tablespoons finely chopped
 flat-leaf parsley

Directions

1. Place the chicken, onion, carrot and celery in a large pan with a lid. Fill with water to cover the chicken, bring to a boil, then immediately turn the heat down to a very gentle bubble.

2. Simmer for about 1 hour until the liquid has reduced by half, skimming off the scum with a large spoon as it comes to the surface (this will help give a good clear stock).

3. Pass the liquid through cheesecloth or a very fine sieve into a smaller pan or bowl and leave to cool. Refrigerate, and preferably the next day remove any fat and sediment which has set on top.

4. Bring the soup gently back to a boil, season well, then add the pasta, cooking until tender. Serve the soup piping hot, garnished with parsley.

Makes 4 servings.

PIGS IN BLANKETS

It's impossible to resist a pig in a blanket. The happiness of hot dogs or sausages wrapped in a sophisticated shell, these treats are perfect for parties and afternoon snacks alike.

Ingredients

1 large egg
1 tablespoon water
1 (14-ounce) package cocktail-size smoked sausage links or hot dogs
¾ cup barbecue sauce
2 (8-ounce) cans refrigerated crescent rolls

Directions

1. Preheat oven to 450°F.

2. In small bowl, beat together egg and water; set aside.

3. Roll out pastries and cut each in half, forming two triangles.

3. Brush sausage links with barbecue sauce.

4. Place one sausage on narrow end of one piece of pastry. Roll to enclose, brushing with egg wash to adhere; transfer to prepared greased baking sheet. Repeat process with remaining sausages and pastry. Brush tops of puff pastry with egg wash.

5. Transfer baking sheet to oven and bake until puffed and golden, about 20 minutes.

Makes about 32 appetizer portions.

FRIED RICE BALLS WITH RED PEPPER SAUCE

Rice plays an integral part in southern farming and cooking. It is a feature of many a meal and any that is left over is always put to good use, either as sweet or savory offerings.

Ingredients

Sauce
2 red bell peppers
2–3 tbsp light vegetable stock
Salt
1–2 teaspoons Tabasco sauce

Rice Balls
2 tablespoons butter
1 small onion, finely chopped
1 green chili, seeded and very
 finely chopped
2 scallions, very finely chopped
12 oz leftover cooked rice
Few saffron strands soaked in 1
 tablespoon boiling water
½ cup flour
Salt
1 teaspoon mustard powder
½ cup cheddar cheese or
 Monterey Jack, finely grated
4 tablespoon cornmeal
1 large egg, beaten
Oil for frying

Directions
1. Halve the bell peppers and roast them until they are blistered and blackened all over. Place them in a plastic bag and leave to cool.

2. Prepare the sauce by removing the skins from the roasted peppers. Process the flesh in a blender with the stock, seasoning and Tabasco sauce, adding extra stock, if necessary, to produce a light pouring consistency. Cover tightly and keep warm.

3. Heat the butter in a small pan and sauté the onion until tender. Add the chili and scallions and cook for another 2 minutes.

4. Put the rice in a large bowl and mix in the onions and chili, the saffron and its liquid, 1 tablespoon of flour, salt, mustard and cheese. When thoroughly mixed, shape into about 20 balls. Chill.

5. Mix the rest of the flour with the cornmeal and put it on a large plate, placing the beaten egg on another. Coat the rice balls with egg, drain off the excess, then coat in the flour and cornmeal mixture. Set aside when well coated, or repeat with any remaining mixture to give a crunchier crust.

6. When ready to serve, heat the oil in a deep-fat fryer to 350F. Shake off any excess coating from the balls and fry three to four at a time for 2 minutes or until golden all over. Remove with a slotted spoon and drain on paper towels.

7. Transfer to a hot plate and keep warm while you cook the rest. Serve with the warm sauce.

Tip: Make smaller versions to serve as tasty bites for a cocktail party.

Makes 4 servings.

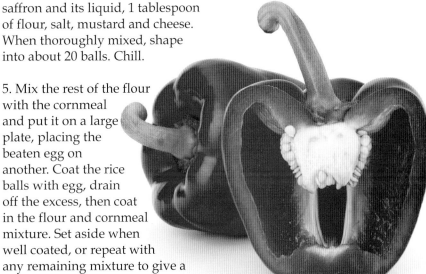

BARBEQUE MEATBALL MINIS

As soon as I had paged through the first cookbook I ever received as a kid, I knew what recipe I wanted to attempt first: meatballs. Meatballs are a great introductory dish for kids, because they're basically a culinary art project. Throw the raw material in a bowl, mix it with the flavorings that make it unique, and then mold it into something with your bare hands (washed well before and after, of course!).

Ingredients
1 pound ground beef
1 small onion, finely chopped
½ cup breadcrumbs
1 large egg, lightly beaten
½ cup 2% milk
1 teaspoon dried parsley
1 teaspoon ground cumin
¼ teaspoon garlic powder
1 teaspoon salt
¾ teaspoon black pepper
1 tablespoon vegetable or olive oil
Barbecue sauce, for serving

Directions
1. In medium bowl, combine beef, onion, breadcrumbs, egg, milk, parsley, cumin, garlic powder, salt, and pepper. Loosely mix together with hands and form into balls about 1 inch in diameter.

2. In large skillet, heat oil over medium-high heat, then add meatballs (in batches if necessary), turning two or three times during cooking, until browned on all sides, about 6–8 minutes.

3. Lower heat to medium and cover. Cook, turning occasionally, until cooked through, about 10 minutes more. Drain on paper towels. Serve with barbecue sauce.

Makes about 20 mini meatballs.

HUSH PUPPIES

The origin of the name "hush puppies" is shrouded in Southern mystery, but the dish itself is straightforward: It's simply fried, seasoned balls of cornmeal. Hush puppies are classically served with fried fish, but also delicious when dipped in tartar sauce, ketchup, or the Spicy Mayo on page 46.

Ingredients
1 cup cornmeal
¼ cup all-purpose flour
1 teaspoon sugar
¾ teaspoon baking powder
¼ teaspoon baking soda
¼ teaspoon salt
⅛ teaspoon black pepper
1 large egg
½ cup buttermilk
¼ cup chopped scallions, white
 and green portions
Vegetable oil, for frying

Directions
1. In large bowl, whisk together cornmeal, flour, sugar, baking powder, baking soda, salt, and pepper.

2. In medium bowl, combine egg and buttermilk and whisk until well-blended. Add scallions.

3. Make a well in cornmeal mixture and pour in egg mixture. Mix until lumps just start to disappear.

4. In large pot, heat enough oil to cover hush puppies over medium-high heat, or set deep-fryer to 375°F. Form tablespoon-sized balls with cornmeal batter. Fry until golden, turning once, about 3 minutes. Drain on paper towels.

Makes 14–18 hush puppies.

SPICY CRAB CAKES

Prepare these the day before and cook them briefly at the last minute when you wish to serve them. These make a great appetizer or a light lunch with a salad; alternatively, they can be made bite-sized for a party buffet.

Ingredients
1 lb crabmeat (fresh, frozen or
  canned)
Salt and black pepper
2 teaspoons chili sauce
1 egg white
1 tablespoon finely chopped
  parsley
1 tablespoon chopped scallions
  (white parts only)
2 tablespoons fine white
  breadcrumbs
2 tablespoons flour
4 tablespoons butter and a little oil
  for frying

Directions
1. In a large bowl, mix the crab with the seasonings, egg white, herbs and breadcrumbs. Combine together very thoroughly. Chill well.

2. Divide the mixture into 10–12 small cakes, dusting each one lightly with flour.

3. Heat half the butter and oil until they bubble and cook half the fish cakes, basting and turning them frequently until they are golden all over (6–7 minutes altogether). Transfer to paper towels to drain while you cook the remainder.

Serve with lemon wedges and mayonnaise.

Makes 10–12 servings.

FRIED PICKLES WITH SPICY MAYO

Fried pickles actually originated in English pubs, but since most Southerners have never met anything they didn't like to fry, they've adopted them as their own. The club soda used in the batter of these crunchy, tangy wonders makes them extra light and crispy. They're great dipped in ranch or blue cheese dressing, but nothing tops homemade spicy mayo!

Ingredients
Spicy Mayo
½ cup mayonnaise
¼–1 teaspoon hot sauce (to taste)
¼ teaspoon seasoned salt
⅛ teaspoon black pepper
Pinch cayenne pepper

Fried Pickles
1 cup all-purpose flour
½ teaspoon baking powder
¼ teaspoon baking soda
½ teaspoon paprika
½ teaspoon salt
⅛ teaspoon black pepper
1 large egg
1 cup club soda
1 (16-ounce) jar dill pickles, quartered
Vegetable or canola oil, for frying

Directions
1. Combine all Spicy Mayo ingredients in bowl and mix well; cover and refrigerate while making Fried Pickles.

2. Heat oil in deep fryer to 350°F, or in large pot over medium-high heat until hot.

3. Drain pickle pieces in colander, then pat with paper towels until dry.

4. Combine flour, baking powder, baking soda, paprika, salt, pepper, and egg. Slowly add club soda and stir with a whisk until well mixed. If batter is too thick, add more club soda as necessary.

5. Dip each pickle slice in batter, then fry until golden brown, about 3–4 minutes. If frying in a skillet, flip with tongs halfway through. Drain on paper towels.

Makes 8–10 appetizer portions.

FRIED JALAPEÑO SLICES

Country cooking is all about frying and spice, and this starter combines both. Pair fried jalapeños with a mild salsa or sour cream and watch them disappear in five minutes flat.

Ingredients

6 fresh jalapeños, sliced ¼-inch thick
½ cup panko breadcrumbs
½ teaspoon garlic powder
½ teaspoon salt
½ teaspoon black pepper
½ cup all-purpose flour, plus more for dredging
2 large eggs, beaten
Vegetable oil, for frying

Directions

1. In large pot, heat oil over medium-high heat, or set deep-fryer to 365°F.

2. In small bowl, mix breadcrumbs, garlic powder, salt, and pepper. In two separate shallow bowls, place flour and beaten eggs.

3. Dip jalapeño slices in flour, then egg, then breadcrumb mixture.

4. Fry, in batches if necessary, until jalapeños float to the surface and are golden brown and crispy. Remove with slotted spoon and drain on paper towels. Repeat with remaining jalapeños.

Makes 5–6 appetizer portions.

GAME-DAY BUFFALO WINGS

For me, football season means only one thing: food. And perhaps no food is more associated with football than buffalo wings. Whether you need something to help you feel better because you're suffering in defeat, or to fuel your winning-streak excitement, any game is better with a plate of these wings in front of you.

Ingredients
Wings
2 pounds chicken wings
2 tablespoons vegetable or olive oil
1½ teaspoons salt
½ teaspoon black pepper

Buffalo Sauce
¼ cup unsalted butter
¼ teaspoon garlic powder
¼ cup hot sauce
½ teaspoon salt
¼ teaspoon black pepper

Directions
1. Preheat oven to 400°F.

2. Pat chicken dry. Toss wings in oil, salt, and pepper, then place on rack, on top of foil-lined baking sheet, and bake on upper oven rack until golden brown and crispy, about 45–50 minutes.

3. While chicken is roasting, melt butter in small saucepan. Add garlic powder, hot sauce, salt, and pepper. Pour sauce in bowl large enough to hold all of chicken and stir to combine.

4. Remove wings from oven, transfer to bowl, and toss with the sauce. Serve warm.

Makes 2–4 servings.

SEAFOOD BITES

Monkfish is perhaps the best choice for this dish as it is a firm fish which keeps its shape and texture during cooking; but any firm white fish would do.

Ingredients
10 oz firm white fish, skinned and
  boned
6 oz large shrimp, peeled and
  deveined
1 cup all-purpose flour
1 tsp easy-blend dried yeast
Salt and pepper
Finely grated rind of 1 lemon
¾ soda water
Oil for deep frying

Directions
1. Cut the fish and shrimp into small pieces.

2. Sift the flour into a bowl. Stir in the yeast, seasoning and lemon rind, and gradually beat in the beer to form a smooth batter. Leave to stand for 15 minutes.

3. Heat the oil in a deep-fryer to 350°F. Dip the fish pieces in the batter and fry for 3–4 minutes until golden brown. Use a slotted spoon to lift them from the pan, then drain them on paper towels.

4. Serve immediately with Spicy Mayo see page 65.

Makes 4 servings.

Scrumptious Salads
& Sides

COUNTRY COBB SALAD

Even if you don't normally like salad, this salad is irresistible – it even has bacon! But what really makes it work is that it's a perfect blend of all different textures – soft crumbled feta cheese, tangy red onion, juciy tomatoes, lettuce, creamy avocado... and did I mention there's bacon?

Ingredients

¼ pound cooked, chopped
  chicken
1 (11- or 12-ounce) bag chopped
  romaine lettuce
5–6 cherry or grape tomatoes,
  chopped
½ small red onion
3 slices bacon, cooked and
  crumbled
¼ cup crumbled feta cheese
1 avocado, chopped
1 large egg, hard-boiled and sliced
¼–⅓ cup ranch or other salad
  dressing

Directions

1. Arrange all the ingredients decoratively over the lettuce.

2. Dress salad according to taste.

Makes 1 main or 4 side salads.

TOMATO & CUCUMBER SALAD

Thanks to its refreshing acidity, this salad is an excellent accompaniment to a meaty or heavy dish like a roast, pasta, or meatloaf.

Ingredients
2 tablespoons Italian dressing
1 cup white vinegar
½ cup sugar
¾ teaspoon salt
3 medium tomatoes, cut into
 wedges
3 medium cucumbers, sliced
½ teaspoon pepper
2 teaspoons chopped fresh dill

Directions
1. In large bowl, mix together Italian dressing, vinegar, sugar, and salt. Stir in tomatoes and sliced cucumbers. Cover and allow to marinate for about an hour before serving.

2. Top with pepper and dill.

Makes 4 servings.

PICNIC POTATO SALAD

You can't have a picnic without potato salad! Well, that might not be true — but why would you want to? Potato salad piled high next to grilled meat is one of the pure joys of summer.

Ingredients

2–3 pounds medium potatoes (about 8), peeled and cubed
1 medium red onion, chopped
2 hard-boiled eggs, chopped
8 sweet pickle chips, chopped
½ cup mayonnaise
3 tablespoons yellow mustard
1 tablespoon sugar
1 teaspoon salt
½ teaspoon black pepper
½ teaspoon paprika

Directions

1. Boil cubed potatoes until tender. Drain and cool.

2. In large bowl, add onion, eggs, pickles, mayonnaise, mustard, sugar, salt, and pepper. Stir well. Fold in drained and cooled potatoes until evenly coated. Chill potato salad at least 2½ hours or overnight.

3. Sprinkle with paprika before serving.

Makes 6 servings.

CHEESY GRITS

You either love them or you don't, but there's perhaps no side dish more Southern than grits. Do them right by adding a healthy amount of cheese.

Ingredients
2 cups water
½ cup quick-cooking grits
1 large egg, beaten
1 cup shredded cheddar cheese
1 tablespoon unsalted butter, plus
 more for serving
½ teaspoon salt

Directions
1. Preheat oven to 325°F.

2. In medium saucepan, heat water to boiling, then slowly add grits while stirring continually.

3. Remove ½ cup grits mixture from pan and add to small bowl with egg. Mix well. Return egg mixture to pan and continue stirring until combined.

4. Remove pan from heat and add cheese, butter, and salt. Stir until well-blended and cheese and butter are melted.

5. Pour grits into 1-quart baking dish. Bake until toothpick inserted in center of grits comes out clean, about 30 minutes. Top with pat of butter and let stand for 5 minutes before serving.

Makes 4 side-dish servings.

COWBOY BEANS

If you were a cowboy cooking a quick meal over an open flame, it wouldn't be too hard to make a variation of this recipe right in the bean can. Luckily you have your stove, but the genius way this recipe quickly makes a cheap can of beans into a side dish just as good as any main dish remains the same.

Ingredients
4 slices bacon
1 large white onion, finely
 chopped
2 jalapeño peppers, seeded and
finely chopped
1 tablespoon tomato paste
1 (29-ounce) can pinto beans,
 rinsed and drained
1 (14.5-ounce) can chicken broth
1 tablespoon light brown sugar
1 teaspoon ground cumin
¾ teaspoon garlic powder
½ teaspoon chili powder
1 teaspoon salt
¾ teaspoon black pepper
¼ cup chopped scallions, for
 garnish

Directions
1. Place bacon in medium skillet, then heat to medium-low. Cook, flipping once, until cooked through and edges start to curl, about 8–12 minutes. Remove to paper towels to drain. When cool, crumble or cut bacon into pieces. Reserve 1 tablespoon bacon fat from skillet.

2. In large pot, heat reserved bacon fat over medium-high heat. Add onion and jalapeños and cook, stirring occasionally, until tender, about 3 minutes.

3. Add tomato paste and mix well to combine. Then add bacon, beans, broth, brown sugar, cumin, garlic powder, chili powder, salt, and pepper and mix well to combine. Heat until bubbling, about 3 minutes, then reduce heat to low and cook, covered, stirring occasionally, until reduced and thickened, about 20–30 minutes. Top with scallions.

Makes 4–6 side dish servings.

FRIED OKRA

You can pick out Southerners in a crowd by whether or not they like okra, a unique vegetable with an inside that can really only be described as "slimy." Frying, however, takes away most of the slimy consistency that's so bizarre to okra newcomers, allowing you to taste okra's unique flavor in this signature Southern dish. If you can't find okra at your supermarket, try at a Caribbean, African, or Mexican market.

Ingredients
½ cup all-purpose flour
½ cup yellow cornmeal
1 tablespoon Creole seasoning
¼ teaspoon garlic powder
1 large egg
1 tablespoon 2% milk
½ pound (2 cups) okra, cut into ½-
  inch pieces
Vegetable oil, for frying

Directions
1. In shallow bowl, combine flour, cornmeal, Creole seasoning, and garlic powder.

2. In separate bowl, whisk together egg and milk.

3. Dip okra pieces in egg mixture, then dredge in flour mixture until well-coated on all sides.

4. In large skillet, heat ¼-inch oil over medium-high heat. Fry okra in batches until golden, flipping once, about 2 minutes per side.

Makes 4 side-dish servings.

COLLARD GREENS & BACON

We have generations of African-American cooks to thank for collard greens, perhaps the most perfect of all side dishes for any country meal. They're tangy, just a bit spicy, and they cut through the grease of meaty main dishes. Meanwhile, they're so packed with green flavor that they almost steal the show.

Ingredients

3 slices bacon
1 large yellow onion, chopped
2 cloves garlic, minced
1 pound fresh collard greens, cut
 into 2-inch pieces
3 cups chicken broth
⅛–¼ teaspoon red pepper flakes
 (to taste)
1 teaspoon salt
1 teaspoon black pepper

Directions

1. Place bacon in medium saucepan, then heat to medium-low. Cook, flipping once, until cooked through and edges start to curl, about 8–12 minutes.

2. Remove bacon to paper towels to drain. Drain all but 1 tablespoon fat from saucepan. Then, add onion.

3. Increase heat to medium-high and cook onion, stirring occasionally, until almost tender, about 3–4 minutes. Add garlic and cook until soft, an additional minute.

4. Crumble bacon and add to saucepan along with collard greens. Cook, stirring continually, until greens start to wilt, about 2–4 minutes.

5. Add chicken broth, red pepper flakes, salt, and pepper. Reduce heat to low, cover, and simmer for 45 minutes, or until greens are tender.

Makes 4 side-dish servings.

ANNUAL GREEN BEAN CASSEROLE

To me, every holiday dinner spread needs a green bean casserole, so I often find myself making it to bring along when invited to Thanksgivings and Christmases at family and friends' homes. One year, after being tasked with bringing other food throughout the holiday season, I realized I had missed my green bean casserole, and made it in the spring. Surprisingly, it didn't seem out of place at all!

Ingredients

1 (10.75-ounce) can
  condensed cream of
  celery soup
¾ cup shredded cheddar
  cheese
½ of 1 (4-ounce) jar pimientos,
  drained and chopped

2 (10- to 12-ounce) packages
  frozen green beans, cooked
¾ cup crunchy French-fried
  onions

Directions

1. Preheat oven to 350°F.

2. In 1½-quart baking dish, combine soup, cheese, and pimientos. Then add green beans and stir until well-combined.

3. Bake, covered, until bubbling, about 20–25 minutes. Uncover and top with French-fried onions and bake for 5 additional minutes.

Makes 6 side-dish servings.

FOUR-CHEESE MAC 'N'CHEESE

Make this gooey, baked mac 'n' cheese and I guarantee your family will ask for it over and over again . . . even if they leave the dinner table with bellies so full they can barely walk!

Ingredients

3 tablespoons unsalted butter
3 tablespoons all-purpose flour
3 cups 2% milk, warmed
½ teaspoon garlic powder
1 teaspoon salt
¾ teaspoon black pepper
½ of 1 (32-ounce) package
 Velveeta cheese
1 cup shredded cheddar cheese,
 divided
½ cup shredded pepper Jack or
 Monterey Jack cheese
½ of 1 (16-ounce) package
 macaroni or ziti noodles, cooked
½ cup grated Parmesan cheese

Directions

1. In medium saucepan, melt butter over medium heat. Add flour and stir constantly over heat until thickened and foamy, about 2 minutes. Slowly stir in milk. Heat, stirring constantly, until thickened, about 5 minutes.

2. Reduce heat to low and add garlic powder, salt, pepper, and Velveeta. Stir until cheese is melted and combined, about 3 minutes. Add half of cheddar and Monterey Jack cheese. Cook, stirring constantly, until cheese melts and is combined, about 5–6 minutes.

3. In lightly greased 11x7-inch casserole dish, pour cheese sauce over noodles and mix until coated. Top with remaining cheddar and Parmesan cheese.

4. Bake in a pre-heated oven at 350°F, uncovered, until top begins to brown for about 30 minutes. Let sit 5 minutes before serving.

Makes 4 side-dish servings.

SOUTHERN SCALLOPED POTATOES

Scalloped potatoes are like mac 'n' cheese taken up a notch, because by cooking the potatoes in the sauce, they become incredibly soft and full of flavor. I love making these scalloped potatoes to accompany a baked ham.

Ingredients

2 tablespoons unsalted butter
1 medium yellow onion, finely
 chopped
1 clove garlic, minced
2 tablespoons all-purpose flour
½ teaspoon salt
¼ teaspoon black pepper
1¼ cups 2% milk
1 cup shredded cheddar cheese,
 divided
1 pound (about 3 medium) white
potatoes, peeled and thinly sliced

Directions

1. Preheat oven to 350°F.

2. In small saucepan, melt butter over medium heat. Add onion and cook until almost tender, about 3 minutes. Add garlic and cook 1 minute more.

3. To same saucepan, add flour, salt, and pepper and stir constantly until thickened, about 1 minute. Slowly add milk, stirring constantly, until thickened, about 3 minutes.

4. Reduce heat to low. Add ¼ cup cheddar cheese and cover with sauce. When melted (about 20–30 seconds), stir to combine. Add remaining cheddar cheese and repeat.

5. Spread small amount of sauce over bottom of lightly greased 1½-quart baking dish. Place half of potatoes, slightly overlapping, on bottom of dish. Cover with half of remaining sauce. Layer remaining potatoes over sauce and top with remaining sauce.

6. Bake, covered, for 45 minutes. Then uncover and bake until potatoes are tender and cheese is bubbly and just starting to brown, about 20–25 minutes more. Let sit for 5 minutes before serving.

Makes 4–6 side-dish servings.

CROWD-PLEASER COLESLAW

When I'm at a barbecue, I expect good grilled meat. But good coleslaw is not always a given. This traditional recipe balances the richness of mayonnaise with the acidity of apple cider vinegar, and is a must-have with ribs, pulled pork, or anything else slathered in sauce.

Ingredients
¾ cup mayonnaise
2 tablespoons sour cream
2 tablespoons yellow onion, finely shredded
1 tablespoon sugar
2 tablespoons apple cider vinegar
1 teaspoon salt
¾ teaspoon pepper
2 large carrots
4 cups (about 1 medium head) shredded green cabbage or coleslaw mix

Directions
1. In large bowl, whisk together mayonnaise, sour cream, onion, sugar, vinegar, salt, and pepper. Mix well to combine.

2. With box grater, grate carrots. Add to bowl along with cabbage. Mix well to combine. Refrigerate for at least 30 minutes before serving.

Makes 8 side-dish servings.

SWEET POTATO CASSEROLE

Marshmallows in a side dish? At Thanksgiving, anything goes! This sweet holiday casserole is right at home on a plate loaded with turkey, stuffing, potatoes, and gravy.

Ingredients

4¼ pounds sweet potatoes
2 tablespoons unsalted butter
½ teaspoon salt
¼ cup light brown sugar
½ teaspoon ground cinnamon
3 cups miniature marshmallows

Directions

1. Preheat oven to 425°F.

2. Place sweet potatoes in shallow baking dish lined with foil. Bake 1 hour or until tender. Reduce oven temperature to 350°F.

3. When cool enough to handle, peel sweet potatoes; place in a large bowl. Add butter, salt, sugar, and cinnamon; mash with potato masher until smooth. Spoon potato mixture into lightly greased 11x7-casserole dish.

4. Bake, covered, for 10 minutes. Uncover and top with marshmallows; bake an additional 10 minutes or until marshmallows are lightly browned.

SWEET POTATO HASH

Sweet potatoes are so American that they were apparently one of the vegetables discovered by Christopher Columbus when landing in the New World. Unlike Sweet Potato Casserole, Sweet Potato Hash is more savory than sweet, thanks to the bell pepper, onion, and my favorite spice, cumin.

Ingredients

1 pound (about 3 medium) sweet potatoes, peeled and cut into small cubes

½ cup water
2 tablespoons olive oil
1 small yellow onion, chopped
½ red or orange bell pepper
1 teaspoon salt
½ teaspoon ground cumin
½ teaspoon black pepper
¼ cup chopped fresh dill
 (optional)
¼ cup chopped scallions
 (optional)

Directions

1. Place sweet potatoes and water in large skillet. Cover and bring to a boil over medium-high heat. Cook for 3 minutes, uncover, and continue cooking until water has evaporated.

2. Move sweet potatoes to side of pan, add oil, and toss to coat. Add onion, pepper, salt, cumin, and pepper, and cook, stirring occasionally, for 5–7 minutes, or until sweet potato is tender and vegetables are golden brown. Stir in dill and scallions, if desired.

Makes 4–6 side-dish servings.

COUNTRY CORN FRITTERS

Food dipped in batter and fried is always delicious, so luckily there's a name for such things: fritters. These fritters are made with corn — use canned or frozen (whatever you prefer), or for a summertime treat, use a fresh-cooked cob with the kernels sliced off.

Ingredients

2 large eggs, beaten
¼ cup all-purpose flour
2 tablespoons grated Parmesan cheese
½ teaspoon salt, plus additional to taste
¼ teaspoon black pepper
2 cups cooked corn
2 scallions, chopped
2 tablespoons vegetable oil

Directions

1. In food processor, pulse eggs, flour, Parmesan cheese, salt, and pepper to combine. Add corn and scallion and pulse 2–3 additional times.

2. In large nonstick skillet, heat oil over medium heat. Working in batches, cook heaping tablespoonfuls of batter until

golden brown, about 4 minutes per side; season fritters with salt.

Makes 4–5 side-dish servings.

SKILLET CORNBREAD

As soon as he heard I had acquired a cast-iron skillet, my mother's cousin Steve had to send me a recipe for skillet cornbread. Purists will tell you the cast iron even imparts an earthy quality to the bread, but I just love how it makes for an incomparably crunchy outside while still leaving the inside moist and fluffy.

Ingredients

½ cup corn oil, divided
2 cups buttermilk
2 large eggs, beaten
2 cups cornmeal
1 tablespoon + ½ teaspoon baking powder
1 teaspoon salt

Directions

1. Coat 10-inch cast-iron skillet with 1 tablespoon oil. Place skillet in oven and preheat to 425°F.

2. In medium bowl, mix together remaining oil, buttermilk, eggs, and cornmeal.

3. Carefully remove hot skillet from oven and reduce oven temperature to 375°F. Pour batter into skillet and place in center of oven. Bake until center is firm and toothpick inserted into center comes out clean, 20–25 minutes. Allow to cool for 10–15 minutes and serve.

Makes 6 servings.

BUTTERMILK BISCUITS

Unlike the flaky biscuits in my recipe for Farm-Style Biscuits and Gravy (page 29), these biscuits are dense and thick, perfect for sopping up gravy or eating alongside soup. For a cheddar biscuit variation, fold in 1½ cups shredded sharp cheddar cheese and 2 teaspoons garlic powder into the batter before baking.

Ingredients
2 cups all-purpose flour
1 tablespoon baking powder
1 teaspoon salt
1 tablespoon sugar
½ cup vegetable shortening
¾ cup buttermilk

Directions
1. Preheat oven to 400°F.

2. In medium bowl, mix flour, baking powder, salt, and sugar together. With a pastry cutter or your fingertips, cut shortening into flour mixture in small pieces.

3. Add buttermilk and stir just until flour mixture is moistened, being careful not to over mix.

4. Turn dough onto floured surface and knead about 20 times.

5. Roll out dough to 1-inch thickness. Using biscuit cutter, cut out biscuits and place them, barely touching, onto a lightly greased or non-stick cookie sheet.

6. Bake for 15 minutes or until golden brown.

Makes 6–8 biscuits.

Hearty Main
Dishes

BARBEQUE BAKED CHICKEN

Believe it or not, the oven is a much better place for barbecued chicken than the grill. Since barbecue sauce contains sugar, it can scorch over a flame, whereas in the oven it slow cooks into a delicious caramelized coating.

Ingredients

3 pounds bone-in chicken parts
1½ cups barbecue sauce
¼ cup peach preserves
1 teaspoon garlic powder
1–3 teaspoons hot sauce (optional)

Directions

1. Preheat oven to 375°F.

2. In large bowl, combine barbecue sauce, preserves, garlic powder, and hot sauce (if desired) and mix well. Remove half of mixture to small bowl or liquid measuring cup and set aside.

3. Add chicken to remaining barbecue sauce mixture in bowl and toss to thoroughly coat.

4. Place chicken in roasting pan or on cookie sheet lined with aluminum foil (using more than one, if necessary), making sure to leave space between each piece.

5. Bake for 15 minutes, then flip over and baste with half of remaining sauce. Continue baking until chicken is cooked through, about 10 more minutes for white meat and 15 more minutes for dark meat.

6. Let cool several minutes before tossing with remaining sauce.

Makes 4–5 servings.

TENNESSEE FRIED CHICKEN

My maternal grandmother is from Tennessee, and this fried chicken recipe was one of the few things she took with her when she left. I still remember trying to see onto the counter as a child, watching impatiently as the chicken came out of the fryer.

Ingredients
1 (3- to 4-pound) chicken, cut into 10 pieces
2 large eggs
1 cup buttermilk
1–2 teaspoons hot sauce
2 cups all-purpose flour
2 teaspoons salt
1½ teaspoons black pepper
¾ teaspoon paprika
Vegetable oil, for frying

Directions
1. In large bowl, whisk eggs, buttermilk, and hot sauce. In separate large bowl, whisk flour, salt, pepper, and paprika.

2. In large pot, heat enough oil to cover chicken over medium-high heat, or heat deep-fryer to 325°F.
3. Pat chicken dry. Working with 1 piece at a time, dredge chicken in flour mixture, then in buttermilk mixture, then again in flour mixture.

4. Working in batches and returning oil to 325°F between batches, fry chicken, turning occasionally, until skin is deep golden brown and crisp, 15–18 minutes. Transfer to paper towels to let drain.

Makes 4–5 servings.

CHICKEN CORDON BLEU

Chicken Cordon Bleu is such a great way to make your average chicken breast seem fancy, it's no wonder it has a chic French name. The ham and cheese elevate these roll-ups into a mouthwatering meal that's anything but "same old."

Ingredients

4 boneless, skinless chicken breasts
4 slices deli ham (¾ ounce each)
4 slices Swiss cheese (¾ ounce each)
1 cup all-purpose flour
¼ cup fresh spinach leaves
1 teaspoon thyme
½ teaspoon salt
¼ teaspoon pepper
2 large eggs, beaten
1 cup seasoned breadcrumbs
1 tablespoon canola oil

Directions

1. Preheat oven to 350ºF.

2. Pound chicken to ¼-inch thickness between two sheets of plastic wrap, then top each breast with a slice of ham, cheese, and three spinach leaves. Roll up and tuck in ends; secure with toothpicks.

3. In shallow bowl, combine flour, thyme, salt, and pepper.

Dip chicken in flour mixture, then in beaten eggs; roll in crumbs.

4. In large skillet, heat oil over medium heat. Brown chicken on all sides. Transfer to 13x9-inch casserole dish coated with cooking spray.

5. Bake, uncovered, for 20–25 minutes or until a thermometer reads 170°F.

Makes 4 servings.

ZESTY ITALIAN CHICKEN BREASTS

This quick and simple recipe was a go-to for my mom, especially when she was working. It's great for a quick dinner, but you can also make a bunch at once and eat them later — I especially like them heated up with pasta, or cold on top of salads.

Ingredients

4 boneless, skinless chicken breasts
1 cup Italian salad dressing, divided
1½ teaspoons salt
1 teaspoon black pepper
1 teaspoon dried thyme, rosemary, or basil
½ teaspoon garlic powder

Directions

1. In small bowl, whisk together salad dressing, thyme (or other herb), and garlic powder.

3. Place chicken in large resealable plastic bag with three-quarters of dressing mixture. Refrigerate in marinade 1–2 hours.

4. Heat barbecue, tabletop grill, or grill pan on high. Place chicken on grill and cook until undersides are browned, 6–8 minutes. Flip and brush with remaining dressing and grill until cooked through, 6–8 minutes more.

Makes 4 servings.

CHICKEN A LA KING

This classic, creamy dish couldn't be simpler. The trick to tender, moist chicken is in the poaching. Keep the water at a bare simmer and remove from the poaching liquid as soon as it's cooked. I like to serve this with rice, but it would be just as tasty over buttered egg noodles or pasta.

Ingredients

4 boneless, skinless chicken
  breasts
1 teaspoon salt
1 tablespoon unsalted butter
½ cup chopped red, orange,
  and/or yellow bell peppers
2 (10.5-ounce) cans condensed
  cream of mushroom soup
1 cup 2% milk
½ teaspoon sweet or smoked
  paprika
¼ teaspoon black pepper
4 cups cooked long-grain white
  rice, for serving
1 tablespoon chopped chives, for
  garnish

Directions

1. In large pot, arrange chicken in single layer (or overlapping very little). Add water until chicken is covered by 1 inch. Sprinkle with salt.

2. Bring water to a boil over medium-high heat, then immediately reduce to a simmer, cover, and cook about 10–12 minutes, or until chicken is cooked through.

3. Remove chicken from poaching liquid and cut into pieces.

4. In large skillet, heat butter over medium heat. Add bell peppers and cook until tender, about 5–7 minutes, stirring often.

5. To same skillet, add soup, milk, paprika, pepper, and chicken; stir and cook until the mixture is hot and bubbling. Serve over rice and sprinkle with chives.

Makes 4 servings.

BACON-WRAPPED GRILLED CHICKEN

Chicken that's dressed to impress — in bacon and fresh rosemary sprigs, to be exact. Throw some baby bell peppers on the grill with them, and you have a meal fit for an adult's sophisticated palate that kids love too.

Ingredients

¼ cup plus 1 tablespoon olive oil, divided
¼ cup lemon juice
2 teaspoons Dijon mustard
1 tablespoon chopped fresh rosemary, plus 8–10 additional sprigs
½ teaspoon garlic powder
½ teaspoon sugar
1 teaspoon salt
¾ teaspoon black pepper
1 pound chicken tenders
½ pound bacon (about 8–10 slices)
10–12 baby bell peppers

Directions

1. In small bowl, whisk together ¼ cup olive oil, lemon juice, mustard, chopped rosemary, garlic powder, sugar, salt, and pepper.

2. In large resealable plastic bag or casserole dish, add chicken and marinade, turning to coat on all sides. Cover and refrigerate for 1 hour.

3. Shake to remove excess marinade from chicken, then wrap each tender in 1 slice bacon and spear with sprig of rosemary to keep bacon in place (use toothpicks if necessary).

4. Heat grill or grill pan over medium-high heat. Coat bell peppers in remaining olive oil.

5. Grill chicken until cooked through, and bacon is crisp, flipping halfway, about 15 minutes. Grill bell peppers until soft, about 2–4 minutes per side.

Makes 3–4 servings.

CHICKEN POT PIE

Chicken pot pie always seems like such a daunting endeavor, especially for a weeknight meal. My version gets this comforting classic on the table in little more than half an hour and is a great way to use up leftover chicken and vegetables. If you want to get fancy, serve them in individual ramekins.

Ingredients

1⅔ cups cooked mixed vegetables or thawed frozen vegetables
1 cup leftover cooked chicken, cut in bite-sized pieces
1 (10.75-ounce) can condensed cream of chicken soup
1 (15-ounce) package refrigerated piecrusts, softened as directed on box

Directions

1. Preheat oven to 425°F.

2. In medium bowl, mix together vegetables, chicken, and soup.

3. Roll 1 piecrust into 13-inch square. Ease into ungreased 9-inch baking dish. Pour chicken mixture into crust-lined dish.

4. Roll remaining piecrust into 11-inch square. Cut out designs with 1-inch cookie cutter. Place square over chicken mixture. Arrange cutouts on top crust. Turn edges of piecrust under; flute edge.

5. Bake about 35 minutes or until golden brown.

Makes 4 servings.

CHICKEN NOODLE CASSEROLE

This recipe is a great example of why I love casseroles — they contain a few simple ingredients that, when thrown together and baked until bubbly — create a whole new taste together. One that you can eat for several meals in a row without getting sick of!

Ingredients

1 tablespoon vegetable or olive oil
2 carrots, peeled and finely
 chopped
½ yellow onion, chopped
½ of 1 (10-ounce) package frozen
 green peas
3 cups cubed cooked chicken
 breasts
1 (16-ounce) jar alfredo sauce
½ teaspoon garlic powder
1 teaspoon salt
¾ teaspoon black pepper
½ of 1 (16-ounce) package
 broad egg noodles, cooked and
 drained
½ cup breadcrumbs
¼ cup grated Parmesan cheese

Directions

1. Preheat oven to 325°F.

2. In large skillet or pot, heat oil over medium-high heat. Add carrot and cook, stirring occasionally, for 3 minutes. Add onion and cook until both vegetables are tender, an additional 3–5 minutes. Add chicken and peas and cook until heated through, about 3 minutes.

3. Remove pan from heat and add alfredo sauce, garlic powder, salt, pepper, and noodles. Mix well. Pour into lightly greased 13x9-inch casserole dish.

4. In small bowl, combine breadcrumbs and cheese, and sprinkle over top of casserole.

5. Bake until bubbly around edges, about 20–30 minutes.

Makes 8 servings.

SPICY CHICKEN MACARONI

Spiced up with jalapeño and pimento, this twist on traditional mac 'n' cheese is anything but tame. Chicken makes it a substantial, belly-filling main, and ricotta cheese adds a rich and creamy texture. If you don't have the twisty cavatappi on hand, feel free to substitute regular elbow macaroni.

Ingredients
½ medium yellow onion, chopped
½ red, yellow, or orange bell
 pepper, chopped
6 ounces button mushrooms,
 chopped
¼ cup unsalted butter
1 (10-ounce) can cream of chicken
 soup
½ of 1 (16-ounce) package
 cavatappi (curly) pasta, cooked
3 cups cubed cooked chicken
½ of 1 (15-ounce) container ricotta
 cheese

1 cup shredded cheddar cheese,
divided

Directions
1. Preheat oven to 350°F.

2. In large skillet, heat oil over medium-high heat, then add onion and bell pepper. Cook 2 minutes, then add mushrooms, and cook until all vegetables are tender, stirring frequently, about 3 minutes more. Stir in soup until well-mixed.

3. In large bowl, combine cavatappi, chicken, ricotta, and ¾ cup cheddar. Mix until well-blended. Fold in soup mixture and mix well.

4. Spoon into lightly greased 9x13-inch casserole dish and bake for 40 minutes.

5. Remove from oven and sprinkle remaining ¼ cup cheese over top of casserole. Return to oven and cook until cheese just begins to turn golden, an additional 15 minutes.

Makes 8 servings.

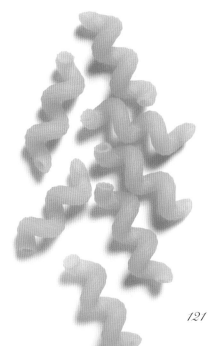

ROASTED CHICKEN & CAULIFLOWER BAKE

A carb-less casserole? It would be nearly impossible without cauliflower, which has a potato-like consistency when it's cooked. Browning cauliflower in the oven makes it taste almost like it was fried, too, making this casserole way healthier than it tastes in more ways than one.

Ingredients

2 tablespoons olive oil
2 heads cauliflower, chopped into florets
2 teaspoons salt, divided
2 cups chopped cooked chicken
1 cup shredded cheddar cheese, divided
1 cup shredded Monterey Jack cheese
½ of 1 (10-ounce) package frozen spinach, thawed and drained

4 slices bacon, cooked and crumbled
½ teaspoon garlic powder
½ teaspoon crushed red pepper flakes
¾ teaspoon black pepper
½ cup Parmesan cheese

Directions

1. Preheat oven to 400°F.

2. On large rimmed baking sheets, toss cauliflower with olive oil and 1 teaspoon salt. Roast, flipping once, until tender and brown, 30–35 minutes. Reduce heat to 350ºF.

3. In large bowl, stir together roasted cauliflower, chicken, ½ cup cheddar cheese, Monterey Jack, spinach, bacon, garlic powder, red pepper flakes, remaining salt, and pepper.

4. Pour into 9x13-inch casserole dish. Top with remaining cheddar and Parmesan cheese. Cover and bake for 25 minutes. Uncover and bake for an additional 10 minutes or until golden brown on top.

Makes 6 servings.

CHICKEN-CORNBREAD CASEROLE WITH A KICK

This casserole is true Southern-Southwestern fusion! It starts with spicy cornbread, and is topped off with cheesy chicken enchilada filling.

Ingredients

1 (8.5-ounce) package corn muffin mix
3 large eggs, beaten
1 (4-ounce) can green chiles, chopped
1 teaspoon baking powder
1 cup sour cream
¼ cup unsalted butter, melted
2½ cups chopped cooked chicken
1 (10-ounce) can enchilada sauce
1½ cups shredded Mexican four-cheese blend
¼ cup chopped fresh cilantro, for garnish

Directions

1. Preheat oven to 350°F.

2. In medium bowl, mix together corn muffin mix, eggs, chiles, baking powder, sour cream, and butter.

3. Pour mixture into lightly greased 11x7-inch casserole dish. Bake 40–45 minutes or until lightly browned. Let sit for 10 minutes.

4. Meanwhile, cook chicken and sauce in pan until heated through. Mix in half of cheese.

5. Spread remaining cheese over cornbread, Pour chicken mixture over cornbread, then top with remaining cheese. Bake for 15–20 more minutes, until cheese has melted and top is light golden brown. Top with cilantro.

Makes 6 servings.

CHICKEN LIVERS WITH ONIONS & WALNUTS

Chicken livers might be an acquired taste for some, but to others, they taste like home. Not only are they super flavorful, but they're also packed with nutrients and vitamins, making them a bona fide superfood.

Ingredients
1 tablespoon butter
2 medium onions, thinly sliced
1 red jalapeño or serrano pepper,
  thinly sliced (optional)
¼ cup coarsely chopped walnuts
¼ teaspoon dried oregano
¼ teaspoon salt
⅛ teaspoon black pepper
1 tablespoon unsalted butter

8 chicken livers
2 tablespoons red wine vinegar
2–3 tablespoons water
Crusty bread or toast, for serving
Garnish with Parsley if desired.

Directions
1. Melt butter in large skillet over medium heat, then add onions and cover Cook, stirring infrequently, until onions are tender and browning, about 20 minutes. If desired, add jalapeño and cook until soft, 5 additional minutes. During last minute of cook time, add walnuts, oregano, salt, and pepper. Remove ingredients from pan and set aside.

2. In same skillet over medium-high heat, add butter. When butter has stopped foaming, add chicken livers and cook, turning, until brown and crisp on both sides but still pink on inside, about 3–4 minutes total. Remove from pan.

3. Return vegetables to pan along with vinegar and 2 or 3 tablespoons water, just enough to deglaze; stir well to combine and serve with livers and crusty bread or toast.

Makes 2-4 servings.

CHICKEN BRUNSWICK STEW

Like many Southern foods, Brunswick Stew has an unknown origin and many different variations depending on what part of the country you're in. It can be made with all kinds of meat, and you'll even find some true country folks making it with squirrel and rabbit. This version, which uses chicken, is most commonly found in Virginia.

Ingredients
1 (3–4 pound) chicken
4 slices bacon
1 medium yellow onion, chopped
1 pound red potatoes, peeled and
  quartered
1 (28-ounce) can tomato puree
1 (14.5-ounce) can diced tomatoes
  with green chiles
¾ cup ketchup
2 tablespoons Worcestershire
  sauce
1 (14.75-ounce) can cream-style
  sweet corn
1 (15.25-ounce) can whole kernel
  corn
2 teaspoons salt
2 teaspoons black pepper

Directions
1. In large pot, place chicken with enough water to cover. Simmer for 2 hours, or until meat is very tender, skimming occasionally. Remove meat to a bowl and reserve stock.

2. Meanwhile, place bacon in medium skillet, then heat to medium-low. Cook, flipping once, until cooked through and edges start to curl, about 8–12 minutes.

3. Remove bacon to paper towels to drain. Drain all but ½ tablespoon of fat from skillet. Then, add onion.

4. Increase heat to medium-high and cook onion, stirring occasionally, until tender, about 5 minutes. Drain any remaining bacon fat.

5. Pull chicken from bone and cut or tear into bite-sized pieces along with bacon.

6. To large pot, add chicken, bacon, onion, 2 pints reserved chicken stock, and remaining ingredients.

7. Cook, stirring occasionally, until flavors are incorporated and potatoes are soft, at least 30 minutes.

Makes 8–10 servings.

CHICKEN & DUMPLING SOUP

Biscuits cooked in simmering chicken broth might be one of the most delicious foods on earth. Serve this rich, thick dish on top of rice or mashed potatoes to transform it from a soup into a delicious gravy.

Ingredients

1 (32-ounce) carton chicken broth (4 cups)

3 cups chopped cooked chicken

2 medium carrots, finely chopped

1 dried bay leaf

½ teaspoon garlic powder

1 (10.75-ounce) can condensed cream of chicken soup

1 (10-ounce) package frozen green peas

½ cup heavy cream

¼ teaspoon dried thyme

1 (16.3-ounce) can refrigerated buttermilk biscuits

1 teaspoon black pepper

1 teaspoon hot sauce (optional)

Directions

1. In large pot, heat broth, chicken, carrots, bay leaf, and garlic powder to boiling over medium-high heat. Reduce heat to low, cover, and simmer 15 minutes, stirring occasionally.

2. Add cream of chicken soup, peas, cream, and thyme. Increase heat to medium-high; return soup to low boil.

3. Cut dough into ½-inch pieces. Drop each piece into simmering soup. Do not stir, but gently move pot in a circular motion so dumplings submerge and cook evenly. Cook until dumplings are floating, 3–4 minutes. Remove bay leaf, and top soup with pepper and hot sauce, if desired, before serving.

Makes 4 servings.

DOWN-HOME CHILI

There's no better comfort food on a winter's night than chili, especially when it's topped with fixin's. This recipe uses Cheddar cheese and scallions, but you can also use sour cream, chopped avocado, or crushed tortilla chips. I prefer to make a batch big enough to last a few days, and change the toppings each night to vary the dish.

Ingredients

1½ pounds ground beef
1 medium red onion, chopped
1 (14.5-ounce) can fire-roasted diced tomatoes
1 (14.5-ounce) can diced tomatoes with green chiles
1 (15-ounce) can small red beans, drained
1 (15-ounce) can kidney beans, drained
1 (14.5-ounce) can beef broth
2 teaspoons dark brown sugar
1 teaspoon garlic powder
1 teaspoon ground cumin
¾–1 teaspoon chili powder
¾ teaspoon dried oregano
⅛ teaspoon cayenne pepper
1 teaspoon salt
1 teaspoon black pepper
½ cup shredded cheddar cheese, for garnish
¼ cup chopped scallions, for garnish

Directions

1. In large pot, heat ground beef over medium heat for 2 minutes. Add onion and cook, stirring occasionally and breaking up meat, until onions are tender and meat is browned, about 6–8 minutes. Drain fat.

2. Increase heat to medium-high. Add all remaining ingredients except cheddar cheese and scallions. Stir well to combine. When chili starts to bubble, reduce heat to low and cover. Simmer, stirring occasionally, until flavors are incorporated and mixture reduces slightly, about 30 minutes.

Makes 8–10 servings.

MAN-APPROVED MEATLOAF

Put this meatloaf in front of a man at dinnertime, and I guarantee his eyes will light up (especially if it's accompanied with a heap of mashed potatoes). If you can't find meatloaf and meatball blend at your supermarket, pure ground beef is just as tasty.

Ingredients

1½ pounds ground meatloaf and
  meatball (beef, veal, and pork)
  blend
1 cup Italian-seasoned
  breadcrumbs
1 medium yellow onion, grated
1 tablespoon Worcestershire sauce
½ teaspoon garlic powder
1 large egg, beaten
2 tablespoons 2% milk
1½ teaspoons salt

¾ teaspoon black pepper
½ cup ketchup
2 tablespoons light brown sugar

Directions

1. Preheat oven to 375°F.

2. In medium bowl, loosely mix together all ingredients except ketchup and brown sugar.

Transfer mixture into lightly greased 9x5-inch loaf pan.

3. Stir together ketchup and brown sugar; brush onto meat. Set pan on rimmed baking sheet, and bake until instant-read thermometer inserted into center reaches 160°F, about 1 hour and 20 minutes. Let cool slightly before serving.

BEEF STEW WITH DUMPLINGS

An excellent family meal that can be prepared a day or two ahead to allow the flavors to mature. For a livelier flavor, add more fresh diced vegetables and herbs towards the end of cooking and before adding the dumplings.

Ingredients
1 tablespoon beef dripping or oil
8 oz button onions, peeled
1½ lb boneless stewing beef, cut into cubes
2 tablespoons flour
3¾ cups beef stock
Salt and freshly ground black pepper
1 clove of garlic, crushed
1 stick of celery, chopped
1 leek
1 cup each chopped carrots and turnips
1 cup ripe tomatoes, peeled and chopped

Dumplings
1 cup all-purpose flour
Good pinch of salt
2 teaspoons baking powder
2 tablespoons chopped mixed fresh herbs
4 tablespoons frozen butter, grated

Directions
1. Heat the fat or oil in a large saucepan and fry the onions until lightly browned. Transfer them to a plate using a slotted spoon. Fry the meat, a few pieces at a time, until brown all over, then remove.

2. Blend the flour into the remaining juices and stir with a wooden spoon until a rich brown color develops. Remove from the heat and, stirring constantly, gradually add the stock, allowing it to return to a boil and thicken.

3. Add the seasoning and garlic, vegetables, the button onions and the meat. Bring back to a boil, cover, and simmer for about 1½ hours.

4. Meanwhile, prepare the dumplings by mixing the flour, salt, baking powder, herbs and grated butter together, adding sufficient cold water to make a soft dough. With wetted hands, form into 10–12 small dumplings, which will swell on cooking.

5. Remove the lid of the saucepan, check the seasonings, and add the dumplings. Bring back to a boil and allow the liquid to gently simmer while the dumplings cook. If the liquid reduces too much, add a little extra hot water and continue to cook until the dumplings have nearly doubled their size.

Makes 4 servings.

BELL PEPPER STUFFED WITH GROUND BEEF & RICE

These sweet juicy, stuffed bell peppers make a vibrant mouth watering dish, served hot or cold.

Ingredients

6 red bell peppers
2 tablespoons olive oil
½ cup chopped onion
½ cup chopped celery
1 lb ground beef
7 oz canned chopped tomatoes
4 tbsp tomato purée
1 clove garlic, crushed
1 teaspoon fresh or dried oregano
1 teaspoon fresh or dried basil
Salt and ground black pepper to taste
1½ cups cooked long grain rice
1 cup cheddar cheese, grated

Directions

1 Prepare the washed peppers by cutting off their tops and removing the seeds. Place in a large, greased baking pan. Chop the edible parts of the removed tops and set them aside.

2 Heat the olive oil in a large skillet over a medium heat until hot. Sauté the chopped pepper

tops, onion and celery for about 5 minutes, or until the vegetables are tender. Add the beef and cook until brown. Add the tomatoes, tomato purée, garlic, oregano, basil and season well. Leave to simmer for about 10 minutes.

3 Add the cooked rice to the mixture and stir well.

4 Stuff the peppers with the beef/rice mixture almost to the top, then bake at 350°F for 55–65 minutes. If desired, top the peppers with a little grated cheddar cheese, then return to the oven until the cheese is melted.

Makes 6 servings.

ULTIMATE BACON BURGERS

If you're going to make a burger to sink your teeth into, why not go all out? These generously sized half-pound burgers are topped with cheese, bacon, and a country-cooking must: buttered buns.

Ingredients
Beef Patties

2 pounds ground beef
2 tablespoons Italian-seasoned breadcrumbs
1 tablespoon barbecue sauce
½ teaspoon liquid smoke
2 teaspoons salt
1 teaspoon black pepper

Burgers

8 slices thick-cut bacon
4 slices American or cheddar cheese
4 hamburger buns
2 tablespoons unsalted butter
1 medium tomato, sliced
½ medium red onion, sliced
4 dill pickles, sliced
Ketchup and/or mustard, for garnish, if desired

Directions

1. Place bacon in large skillet, then heat to medium-low. Cook, flipping once, until cooked through and edges start to curl, about 8–12 minutes. Remove bacon to paper towels to drain. Set aside.

2. Preheat lightly oiled or seasoned cast-iron grill pan on high. Meanwhile, in large bowl, mix meat with remaining burger ingredients. Form into 4 patties.

3. Add patties to pan in batches, leaving space between each. Press into grill pan with spatula. Flip after 5 minutes. Cook another 5 minutes for medium-rare to medium, or to desired doneness. Add cheese 2 minutes before end of cook time.

4. Butter buns and toast. Top with desired condiments like ketchup and/or mustard, then bacon, tomato, onion, and pickles.

Makes 4 servings.

TATER TOT CASSEROLE

This casserole proves that tater tots are not just for kids, though kids do love them. If your kids are picky eaters, add cooked and chopped carrots, celery, or even spinach to sneak some vegetables into their diets!

Ingredients

1½ pounds ground beef
1 medium yellow onion, chopped
1 (10-ounce) package frozen green peas
¼ cup steak sauce
1 tablespoon Worcestershire sauce
3 ounces cream cheese
½ teaspoon garlic powder
⅛ teaspoon cayenne pepper (optional)
1 teaspoon salt
¾ teaspoon black pepper
1 cup shredded cheddar cheese
½ of 1 (32-ounce) package tater tots

Directions

1. Preheat oven to 450°F.

2. In large pot, heat ground beef over medium-high heat, stirring occasionally and breaking up meat until browned, about 5–7 minutes. Remove meat to covered dish and set aside. Drain all but 1 tablespoon fat from pot.

3. Add onion and cook, stirring occasionally, until tender, about 3–5 minutes.

4. Add peas, steak sauce, Worcestershire, cream cheese, garlic powder, cayenne (if using), salt, and black pepper.

5. Cook, stirring, over low heat until cream cheese is melted and peas are cooked through, about 3 minutes. Add reserved meat and stir to mix.

6. Pour meat mixture into 9x13-inch casserole dish. Top with cheese.

7. Arrange tater tots in single layer over top of cheese. Bake uncovered until tots are golden, about 20–30 minutes.

Makes 8 servings.

TEX-MEX CASSEROLE

It's partly because America shares a border with Mexico, of course, but one of the big reasons Mexican ingredients have found their way into country cooking is because they share big flavors with plenty of spice. This dish combines ground beef, beans, and corn with lasagna noodles for a fusion of textures as well as cultures.

Ingredients

1 pound ground beef
1 medium yellow onion, chopped
1 (10-ounce) package frozen corn
1 (15-ounce) can kidney beans, drained
1 (14.5-ounce) can diced tomatoes with green chiles
½ teaspoon garlic powder
½ teaspoon chili powder
1 teaspoon salt
¾ teaspoon black pepper
½ of 1 (16-ounce) package lasagna noodles, cooked
2 cups shredded Mexican four-cheese blend

Directions

1. Preheat oven to 350°F.

2. In large skillet, heat ground beef over medium-high heat, stirring occasionally and breaking up meat, 3 minutes. Add onion and cook until meat is browned and onion is tender, about 5 minutes more.

Add corn and cook for 1 minute. Drain fat, then stir in kidney beans, tomatoes, and spices.

4. In lightly greased 11x7-inch casserole dish, layer noodles, then one-third of meat mixture, then one-third cheese. Repeat until meat mixture is used up.

5. Bake, covered in aluminum foil, for 30 minutes, then uncover and continue baking for 15 minutes, until cheese on top just starts to turn golden.

Makes 4–6 servings.

CHICKEN-FRIED STEAK

There's no actual chicken in chicken-fried steak, just the deliciousness of fried chicken in a crunchy coating and chicken-broth gravy. A variation of this dish is called country-fried steak, which uses a beef gravy and omits the eggs.

Ingredients
Steak
2 pounds cube steak or bottom
 beef round, pounded to ¼-inch
 thickness
1 teaspoon salt
1 teaspoon black pepper
3 large eggs, beaten
¼ cup 2% milk
1 cup all-purpose flour
Canola or vegetable oil, for frying

Gravy
3 tablespoons all-purpose flour
2 cups chicken broth
½ cup 2% milk
1/8 teaspoon dried thyme
½ teaspoon salt (optional)
¼ teaspoon black pepper
 (optional)

Directions
Steak
1. Season meat on both sides with salt and pepper.

2. In large shallow bowl, whisk together eggs and milk. In separate shallow bowl, add flour.

3. Working with one piece at a time, dredge steak in flour. Turn to coat, shaking off excess. Place meat in egg mixture, turning to coat, then dredge again in flour. Repeat with remaining steaks.

4. In large skillet, heat ¼ inch oil over medium heat. Cook steak, in batches if necessary, until edges are golden brown, 2–3 minutes per side. Remove steaks to paper towel–lined plate and keep warm by tenting with foil. Repeat until all steaks are cooked.

Gravy
1. Drain all but 1 tablespoon fat from skillet. Whisk in flour. Add broth and whisk until gravy comes to a boil and begins to thicken.

2. Add milk and thyme and whisk 5–10 minutes, or until gravy reaches desired thickness. Season to taste with salt and pepper, if desired. Serve gravy over steaks.

Makes 4–6 servings.

SUNDAY ROAST

It doesn't have to be a special occasion to gather family and friends for a great meal – and it doesn't have to be hard to prepare either. You just need a great piece of meat, a simple rub, and some roasting time. Have someone else bring the sides and dinner is done!

Ingredients

1 5-pound bone-in or boneless
 prime rib roast
1 tablespoon olive oil
1 tablespoon salt
1 tablespoon black pepper
1 teaspoon dried chopped
 rosemary
½ teaspoon dried thyme
½ teaspoon garlic powder

Directions

1. At least two hours before cooking, rub roast with olive oil, sprinkle with spice blend, and refrigerate.

2. Preheat oven to 450°F. At least 30 minutes before cooking, remove roast from refrigerator and allow to come to room temperature.

3. Place roast in high-sided roasting pan bone-side down. Roast for 15 minutes, then reduce oven temperature to 325°F and continue to cook until meat thermometer inserted in center reads 110°F, about 15 minutes per pound of meat.

4. Remove from oven and let rest for 20 minutes. The roast will continue to cook as juices redistribute, raising the internal temperature to 130°F for medium-rare.

Makes 10–12 servings.

SHERRI'S BEEF STROGANOFF

Beef stroganoff isn't from the American South, but my friend Sherri is. Her beef stroganoff also has an unmistakably American ingredient — cream of mushroom soup. This shortcut gives the sauce a complex flavor without a lot of work. Make it even less work by substituting ground beef for cubed and cutting the cooking time by an hour!

Ingredients

½ teaspoon garlic powder
1½ teaspoons salt
¼ teaspoon black pepper
2 pounds beef chuck, trimmed of excess fat and cut into bite-sized pieces
⅓ cup plus 3 tablespoons all-purpose flour, divided
2 tablespoons canola oil
1 large yellow onion, sliced
1 tablespoon Worcestershire sauce
2 (14.5-ounce) cans beef broth
1½ tablespoons unsalted butter, divided
1 (8-ounce) package cremini mushrooms, sliced
½ cup sour cream
1 (16-ounce) package egg noodles, cooked
3 tablespoons chopped fresh parsley, for garnish

Directions

1. In large bowl, mix together garlic powder, salt, and pepper. Pat beef dry with paper towels and add to bowl; toss to coat. Add ⅓ cup flour and toss again.

2. In large pot, heat oil over medium-high heat. Working in batches, add beef and cook until browned on all sides, about 5 minutes per batch. Set aside. Reduce heat to medium and add onion. Cook, stirring often, until fragrant and starting to soften, about 2 minutes.

3. Add Worcestershire and beef broth and cook, scraping up any brown bits with spoon. 4. Return meat to pot and bring to a simmer. Reduce heat to low, cover, and simmer, stirring occasionally, until beef is almost tender, about 1½ hours.

5. Transfer 1 cup broth to small bowl; add remaining 3 tablespoons flour and whisk until smooth. Stir flour mixture into pot.

6. In large skillet, melt ½ tablespoon butter over medium heat. Add mushrooms and cook, stirring often, until golden brown, 5–7 minutes. Add mushrooms to meat mixture and continue to simmer until meat is tender, about 30 minutes longer. Stir in sour cream and season to taste.

7. Meanwhile, toss cooked egg noodles with remaining tablespoon butter. Place buttered egg noodles in large bowl and spoon the beef over them. Garnish with parsley.

Makes 8 servings.

COUNTRY LAMB CHOPS

Lamb chops are a great way to shake up a weekday dinner routine. Pop some potatoes in the oven before you start marinating the lamb and you'll have baked potatoes and lamb chops all ready with about 15 minutes of prep time.

Ingredients

3 tablespoons olive oil, divided
1 teaspoon garlic powder
½ teaspoon paprika
¼ teaspoon dried oregano
⅛ teaspoon cayenne pepper
2 teaspoons salt
½ teaspoon black pepper
6 1¼-inch-thick lamb loin chops

Directions

1. Preheat oven to 400°F.

2. In large bowl, mix all ingredients but lamb chops and 1 tablespoon olive oil. Add lamb; turn to coat. Marinate at room temperature at least 30 minutes and up to 1 hour.

3. In large, ovenproof skillet over high heat, heat remaining tablespoon olive oil. Add lamb; cook until browned, about 3–4 minutes per side.

4. Place skillet in oven and cook lamb chops until desired doneness, about 10 minutes for medium-rare. Let sit for 5 minutes before serving.

Makes 6 servings.

LAMB ROAST WITH POTATOES

The great thing about a lamb loin is that it takes half the time of a pork loin. However, if you can't find a lamb loin, you can still use pork. Just cook it for about 50–60 minutes, and don't add the vegetables until halfway through the cooking time.

Ingredients

5 white potatoes, quartered
12 baby carrots
1 medium yellow onion, coarsely
 chopped
4 cloves garlic, peeled
2 pounds loin of lamb, fat on
1 tablespoon olive oil
1 tablespoon salt
2 teaspoons black pepper

Directions

1. Preheat oven to 400°F.

2. Bring large pot of water to the boil, add potatoes, and simmer until almost tender, 7–8 minutes. Drain thoroughly and leave to cool for 10 minutes.

3. Add potatoes, carrots, onion, and garlic to roasting pan.

4. Rub lamb with oil and season with salt and pepper.

5. In large skillet over medium-high heat, sear meat on all sides until golden-brown, about 3 minutes per side.

6. Remove from heat and place loin on top of chopped vegetables. Roast for 20–25 minutes for medium-rare, stirring the vegetables once during roasting.

7. Let lamb rest for at least 15 minutes, covered in foil, before carving.

Makes 6 servings.

PORK RIBS WITH HONEY BARBEQUE SAUCE

Country cooking may be about a lot of things, but country eating is all about getting your fingers dirty. These pork ribs with sticky honey barbecue sauce will definitely do the trick. Serve with fries or another finger food so you don't have to touch a fork!

Ingredients

1 tablespoon light brown sugar
2 teaspoons garlic powder
2 teaspoons ground cumin
1 teaspoon chili powder
1 teaspoon paprika
⅛ teaspoon cayenne pepper
2 teaspoons salt
1 teaspoon black pepper
2 (2-pound) racks pork spareribs
¼ cup barbecue sauce
1 tablespoon honey

Directions

1. Preheat oven to 400°F. Remove membrane from back of rib racks.

2. In small bowl, combine brown sugar, garlic powder, cumin, chili powder, paprika, cayenne, salt, and black pepper. Rub all over ribs with fingers.

3. Place rib racks side-by-side (meaty side up) and wrap tightly

with aluminum foil. Place on baking sheet and cook until tender, 1½–2 hours.

4. In small bowl, mix barbecue sauce and honey.

5. Set oven to broil. Open aluminum foil packet and brush barbecue sauce mixture on ribs. Place under broiler until barbecue sauce turns darker and starts to bubble, about 3–5 minutes.

Makes 4 servings.

CAROLINA PULLED PORK SANDWICHES

There's so much to love about these slow-roasted sandwiches that are perfect for picnics and other big gatherings. They may take a lot of cooking time, but they're simple to construct, very inexpensive, and packed with flavor. The Carolina-style "sauce" is more like dressed-up vinegar, and it's my favorite for pulled pork because it doesn't add heaviness. Instead, its acidity balances out any greasiness in the rich meat while adding moisture and a hint of flavor.

Ingredients
Sandwiches

2 teaspoons ground cumin
2 teaspoons garlic powder
1 teaspoon chili powder
½ teaspoon paprika
1 teaspoon salt
½ teaspoon black pepper
1 (6–8 pound) bone-in pork
 shoulder
16–20 hamburger buns

Sauce

1½ cups apple cider vinegar
½ cup ketchup
1/3 cup dark brown sugar
1 tablespoon red pepper flakes
1½ tablespoons salt
2 teaspoons black pepper

Directions

1. Preheat oven to 450°F.

2. In small bowl, combine cumin, garlic powder, chili powder, paprika, salt, and pepper.

3. Pat pork dry, then rub spice mixture on all exposed meat (not the skin). Place skin-side-up in roasting pan.

4. Cook for 20 minutes, then reduce heat to 325°F and cook 1 hour for every pound of meat, about 6–8 hours. An instant-read thermometer should read 185°F when inserted in center of meat, and meat should easily fall away from the bone. Remove pork from oven and let rest 20–30 minutes.

5. Meanwhile, in large bowl, combine Sauce ingredients and mix until sugar and salt have dissolved. Cover and set aside.

6. When pork is cool enough to handle, remove from bone and pull apart with your fingers. Thoroughly mix when finished, to evenly distribute the various textures of meat.

7. Add pulled pork to clean roasting pan and stir in sauce. Cook, covered with foil, until warm and steaming, about 15 minutes. Serve on hamburger buns.

Makes 16–20 sandwiches.

PORK CHOPS WITH MUSHROOM GRAVY

These pork chops were a regular at my dinner table growing up. Even if you've never had them, they still might taste like home!

Ingredients

1 tablespoon vegetable or olive oil
4 (½-inch-thick) boneless pork
 cutlets
1 teaspoon salt
¾ teaspoon black pepper

1 (10.75-ounce) can condensed
 golden mushroom soup
¼ cup 2% milk
1 teaspoon Worcestershire sauce
¼ teaspoon garlic powder
½ teaspoon black pepper

Directions

1. In large skillet, heat oil over medium-high heat. Sprinkle salt and pepper on both sides of pork cutlets. Add pork culets to skillet and cook, flipping once, until browned (but not cooked through), about 3–5 minutes per side.

2. Add soup, milk, Worcestershire sauce, garlic powder, and pepper. When mixture begins to bubble, reduce heat to low.

3. Cook, covered, until pork is cooked through, about 3–4 minutes.

Makes 4 servings.

APPLE-SMOTHERED PORK CHOPS

This recipe uses thicker, bone-in chops than the Pork Chops with Mushroom Gravy. Their preparation is a bit fancier too — topped with caramelized onions and warm apples, their rustic flavor will remind you of fall.

Ingredients

1 tablespoon vegetable or olive oil
4 (¾-inch-thick) bone-in pork chops
1 teaspoon salt
¾ teaspoon black pepper
2 tablespoons unsalted butter
1 medium white onion, sliced
3 semi-tart apples like Braeburn, Cortland, or Honeycrisp, cored and chopped
1 cup apple juice or water

Directions

1. In large skillet, heat oil over medium-high heat. Sprinkle salt and pepper on both sides of pork chops. Add pork chops to skillet and cook, flipping once, until browned (but not cooked through), about 3–5 minutes per side. Set aside, covered.

2. In skillet, melt butter. Add onions and apples and cook, stirring occasionally, until onion slices have started to brown and apples are almost soft, about 8 minutes. Add apple juice or water and stir well to combine.

3. Return pork chops to skillet and cook until tender, about 8–12 minutes, turning halfway. Serve chops with apple-onion mixture on top.

Makes 4 servings.

ROSEMARY & THYME PORK ROAST

If it were economical, I might make this pork roast every week. Still, it's a matchless dinner for a holiday or special occasion, especially when paired with the Sweet Potato Hash on page 97.

Ingredients
½ cup olive oil
½ cup apple cider vinegar
2 teaspoons Dijon mustard
½ teaspoon dried thyme
½ teaspoon dried rosemary
¼ teaspoon garlic powder
1½ teaspoons salt
1 teaspoon black pepper
1 (2-pound) boneless pork loin
 roast

Directions
1. Preheat oven to 350°F.

2. In small bowl, mix all ingredients except pork loin. Pour mixture into resealable plastic bag and add pork loin, turning to coat. Push all air out of bag and seal. Refrigerate for at least 4 hours and up to overnight.

3. Remove pork from marinade, shaking off excess, and place in shallow baking pan and cook, uncovered, until tender, about 1 hour. Let sit for 10 minutes before serving.

Makes 4–5 servings.

HOPPIN' JOHN WITH PORK

Black-eyed peas, which are actually beans, are one of the most widely grown crops in the South. So naturally, they have to have their own dish! The origins of the term "Hoppin' John" are unknown, but the dish has been around almost as long as America itself.

Ingredients

1 tablespoon vegetable or olive oil
4 (¼- to ½-inch-thick) pork
  tenderloin medallions, trimmed
  and sliced into bite-sized pieces
3 stalks celery, chopped
1 medium yellow onion, chopped
1 jalapeño, seeded and finely
  chopped
2 (28-ounce) cans black-eyed peas,
  drained and rinsed
1 cup chicken broth
½ teaspoon garlic powder
1 bay leaf
1 teaspoon salt
¾ teaspoon black pepper
¼ cup chopped scallions
2 cups long-grain rice, cooked
(for serving)

Directions

1. In large pot, heat oil over medium-high heat. Add pork and cook, stirring frequently, until golden brown on all sides, about 5 minutes.

2. Add celery, onion, and jalapeño. Cook, stirring occasionally, until vegetables are tender, about 5 minutes, then add chicken broth, garlic powder, bay leaf, salt, and pepper.

3. Reduce heat to low and cook, covered, until heated through, about 8–10 minutes. Remove bay leaf. Top with scallions and serve over rice.

Makes 6 servings.

HAM & CHEESE CASSEROLE

This cheesy casserole is perfect for using leftover ham, but if you don't have any on hand, simply buy a pound at the butcher counter and ask them not to slice it.

Ingredients
½ medium yellow onion, chopped
½ red bell pepper, chopped
½ cup sour cream
2 tablespoons mayonnaise
1 large egg
1 teaspoon Dijon mustard
½ teaspoon garlic powder
¼ teaspoon ground thyme
1 teaspoon salt
¾ teaspoon black pepper
½ of 1 (16-ounce) package
 cavatappi (curly) pasta, cooked
1 pound (about 3 cups) ham,
 chopped

1½ cups shredded cheddar cheese, divided

Directions
1. Preheat oven to 350°F.

2. In large skillet, heat oil over medium-high heat, then add onion and bell pepper. Cook, stirring occasionally, until tender, about 5 minutes.

3. In large bowl, combine sour cream, mayonnaise, egg, mustard, garlic powder, thyme, salt, and pepper. Mix well to combine. Add onion–bell pepper mixture, pasta, ham, and half of cheddar cheese. Mix well to combine.

4. Pour into lightly greased 9x13-inch casserole dish. Top with remaining cheese. Bake uncovered until cheese is bubbly, about 40 minutes.

Makes 6–8 servings.

SAUSAGE CALZONES

Calzones began in the country kitchens of Italy, and when they migrated to the United States, they got bigger (and, probably, cheesier). Use refrigerated dough from your supermarket, or ask at your favorite independent pizza parlor for a round of theirs. Most pizza shops will sell you uncooked dough for a few dollars.

Ingredients

½ teaspoon vegetable or olive oil
1 pound bulk Italian sausage
1 cup whole-milk ricotta cheese
1 cup shredded mozzarella cheese
¼ teaspoon dried oregano
¼ teaspoon dried basil
½ teaspoon garlic powder
⅛ teaspoon cayenne pepper
½ teaspoon salt
¼ teaspoon black pepper
1 (16-ounce) round refrigerated
 pizza dough
1 large egg, beaten
Pizza sauce or marinara sauce,
 for serving

Directions

1. Heat oven to 375°F.

2. In medium skillet, heat oil over medium-high heat, then add sausage. Cook, stirring to break up and turn meat, until browned, about 5–7 minutes. Remove from heat and add cheeses, oregano, basil, garlic powder, cayenne, salt, and black pepper. Stir to combine.

3. Divide dough into 8 sections and roll into balls, then flatten each ball into a circle. Place meat mixture onto one half of each of circle, leaving a ½-inch border around the edge. Fold dough over filling, then press edges of dough together with tines of a fork to seal.

4. Place calzones on lightly greased baking sheet and brush tops with egg. Prick tops with fork to allow steam to escape.

5. Bake 20–22 minutes or until dough is golden brown. Cool 10 minutes on cookie sheet. Serve with warmed marinara sauce.

Makes 4 servings.

CAJUN SAUSAGE & RICE

Known throughout Louisiana as "red beans and rice" and sometimes made with a ham hock or bacon, this dish is perfect for filling empty bellies at dinnertime.

Ingredients

½ tablespoon vegetable or olive oil
1 pound hot or sweet sausage
3 stalks celery, chopped
1 medium yellow onion, finely
  chopped
½ cup water
2 bay leaves
½ teaspoon garlic powder
½ teaspoon paprika
1 teaspoon salt
¾ teaspoon black pepper
⅛ teaspoon cayenne pepper
2 (15-ounce) cans small red beans
2 cups cooked rice, for serving

Directions

1. In large skillet over medium heat, heat oil, then add sausage and cook until browned, 3–4 minutes.

2. Add celery and onion. Continue to cook until vegetables are tender, about 5–6 minutes, then stir in water, bay leaves, garlic powder, paprika, salt, black pepper, cayenne, and beans.

3. Lower heat, cover, and simmer for 15–20 minutes. Remove bay leaves. Serve over hot rice.

Makes 4–6 servings.

NEW ORLEANS JAMBALAYA

New Orleans is known for its seafood and its spicy Andouille sausage, and this one-pot meal has both. An American version of Spanish paella, the rice cooks with the broth and other ingredients to make it the tastiest rice you'll ever eat.

Ingredients

1 tablespoon vegetable or olive oil
1 pound Andouille sausage, sliced ¼-inch thick
1 pound frozen shrimp, thawed
1 medium yellow onion, chopped
1 celery stalk, chopped
½ of 1 red bell pepper, chopped
1 bay leaf
½ teaspoon garlic powder
½ teaspoon dried oregano
1 teaspoon salt
¾ teaspoon black pepper
¼ teaspoon cayenne pepper
2 (10.5-ounce) cans chicken broth
1 (14.5-ounce) can diced tomatoes
1 cup long-grain rice

Directions

1. In large skillet over medium-high heat, heat oil, then add sausage; cook, stirring occasionally, 5 minutes, until browned. Add shrimp and cook until cooked through, about 2 minutes. Remove from skillet.

2. Reduce heat to medium. Add onion, celery, bell peper and cook, stirring occasionally, for 2 minutes or until onion is softened. Stir in bay leaf, garlic powder, oregano, salt, black pepper, and cayenne. Return shrimp and sausage to skillet.

3. Stir in broth and tomatoes; bring to boil, then stir in rice. Reduce heat to low; cover and cook 20–25 minutes or until rice is tender. Remove bay leaf.

Makes 4–5 servings.

175

EASY GUMBO

Gumbo is a bit like a soup version of jambalaya, and it usually takes a lot of time at the stove to get a perfectly browned roux (flour and fat mixture) for its base. In this recipe, the roux is made in the oven, making it the easiest from-scratch gumbo recipe you'll ever try.

Ingredients

½ cup + 1 tablespoon vegetable oil, divided
⅔ cup all-purpose flour
½ pound Andouille sausage, cut into ¼-inch pieces
2 small yellow onions, finely chopped
2 stalks celery, finely chopped
½ of 1 green bell pepper, finely chopped
1½ teaspoons garlic powder
1 (15-ounce) can diced tomatoes
1 tablespoon Worcestershire sauce
2 teaspoons Creole seasoning
½ teaspoon ground thyme
¼ teaspoon cayenne pepper
1 tablespoon salt
½ teaspoon black pepper
2 bay leaves
½ pound okra (about 1 cup), chopped
2 quarts chicken broth, warmed
1½ cups cooked chopped chicken

Directions

1. Preheat oven to 350°F.

2. In large, oven-safe pot, whisk together ½ cup oil and flour. Place on middle rack of oven, uncovered, and bake for 1½ hours, whisking 2–3 times throughout the cooking process.

3. While roux is baking, heat remaining oil in medium skillet over medium-high heat. Add sausage and stir occasionally, until browned, about 5 minutes. Set aside.

4. Once roux is done, carefully remove pot from oven and set over medium-high heat. Add onion, celery, bell pepper, and garlic powder and cook, stirring frequently, until onion begins to turn translucent, about 7 minutes.

5. Add tomatoes, Worcestershire sauce, Creole seasoning, thyme, cayenne, salt, black pepper, bay leaves, and okra and stir to combine.

6. Gradually add chicken broth while whisking continually. Decrease heat to low, cover, and cook for 35 minutes. Remove from heat, add chicken and sausage, and stir to combine. Remove bay leaf. Serve over rice.

Makes 6 servings.

CREOLE-SPICED SHRIMP

Fresh shrimp are so tasty they don't need much to make them mouthwatering. But this spicy preparation is so good, you'll never want them any other way. Serve the shrimp over white rice or, more traditionally, cheesy grits like the ones from page 79.

Ingredients

1 tablespoon bacon grease, other meat drippings, or butter
1 pound fresh large shrimp, peeled and deveined
1½ teaspoons creole seasoning
½ teaspoon salt
¼ teaspoon black pepper
½–1 teaspoon hot sauce
¼ cup chopped fresh chives or scallions
¼ cup shredded cheddar cheese
½ tablespoon cooking oil

Directions

1. Heat the bacon grease in a large skillet over medium-low heat.

2. Add shrimp and cook 1 minute on each side. Add the creole seasoning, hot sauce, salt, and pepper; cook 2 minutes, stirring until the shrimp are coated and cooked through. Sprinkle with chives and cheese.

Makes 3–4 servings.

PANFISH

Country cooks don't agree on everything, but we do agree that fish should always be fried. Serve with ketchup or tartar sauce for dipping and include some hush puppies (see page 75) for true Southern authenticity.

Ingredients

¼ cup sesame seeds
1 cup yellow cornmeal
1 cup all-purpose flour
1 teaspoon paprika
½ teaspoon garlic powder
1 teaspoon salt
¾ teaspoon black pepper
2 pounds boneless panfish fillets, such as perch, white bass or sunfish cut into 1-inch strips
Vegetable oil, for frying

Directions

1. In large skillet over medium-low heat, add sesame seeds and cook, stirring frequently, until they start to smell nutty, about 2 minutes. Remove from skillet and set aside. Add oil to fill skillet halfway, and heat over medium-high.

2. In shallow bowl, combine cornmeal, flour, paprika, garlic powder, salt, and pepper.

3. Pat fish dry with paper towels. Then dredge in cornmeal mixture on all sides, coating evenly.

4. Add fish (in batches if necessary) to hot oil and fry until golden brown, flipping once, about 7–8 minutes. Sprinkle with sesame seeds before serving.

Makes 4 servings.

UNCLE JIM'S SALMON BURGER

My Uncle Jim, a triathlete, is always trying to get us to eat healthier. (He's also been accused of stuffing vegetables into our food without our knowledge.) These salmon burgers — easy to make in a food processor — are so delicious, your family might actually request them over regular burgers!

Ingredients

1 pound fresh salmon, skin
  removed
1 tablespoon Dijon mustard
2 tablespoons mayonnaise
1 tablespoon lemon juice
1 large shallot, finely chopped
¼ teaspoon hot sauce
1 teaspoon salt
¾ teaspoon black pepper
1 cup panko breadcrumbs,
  divided
2 tablespoons olive oil
4 kaiser buns
¼ cup tartar sauce, for serving
2 medium tomatoes, sliced, for
  serving
½ medium red onion, sliced, for
  serving
Lettuce, for serving

Directions

1. Chop three-quarters of salmon into ¼-inch pieces. Put in large bowl and set aside.

2. Cut remaining salmon into large pieces and place in food processor bowl along with mustard, mayonnaise, lemon juice, shallots, hot sauce, salt, and pepper. Pulse to make a paste.

3. Add pureed salmon mixture to bowl with chopped salmon. Add 2 tablespoons panko. Gently mix until just combined.

4. Divide salmon into four equal parts and form into patties. Cover with plastic wrap and refrigerate 30–60 minutes.

5. Spread remaining panko on a plate. Press both sides of salmon patties in panko.

6. In large nonstick or cast-iron skillet, heat olive oil over medium-high heat. Add patties (in batches if necessary) and cook until browned on bottom, 3–4 minutes. Turn and cook until other side is browned and patties are springy in center, 3–4 more minutes. Transfer to paper towels to drain.

6. Place on buns and top with tartar sauce, tomatoes, onions, and lettuce.

Makes 4 servings.

GROWN-UP FISH STICKS

Fish sticks don't just have to be for kids! White fish is easy to find, inexpensive, and good for you. So why not fry it up for dinner?

Ingredients

1½ pounds white fish fillets (such as cod or tilapia), each about ¾-inch thick
1 cup all-purpose flour
½ teaspoon baking powder
¼ teaspoon baking soda
¼ teaspoon dried parsley
½ teaspoon salt
¼ teaspoon black pepper
⅛ teaspoon cayenne pepper
1 cup club soda
1 large egg
Vegetable oil, for frying

Directions

1. Heat oil in deep fryer to 360°F, or in large pot over medium-high heat until hot.

2. Pat fish with paper towels until fully dry and cut into 1-inch long strips.

3. In medium bowl, combine flour, baking powder, baking soda, parsley, salt, black pepper, cayenne, and egg. Slowly add club soda and whisk until well mixed.

If batter is too thick, add more club soda as necessary.

4. Dip each piece of fish in batter, then fry until golden brown, about 5 minutes. If frying in a pot, flip with tongs halfway through. Drain on paper towels.

Makes 4 servings.

TUNA NOODLE CASSEROLE

Nothing says country potluck like Tuna Noodle Casserole. You can't beat its comfort-food factor, and it's easy to make with some cans of tuna you bought on sale and forgot in the back of your cupboard.

Ingredients

½ of 1 (16-ounce) package elbow
 macaroni noodles, cooked
1 (10.75-ounce) can cream of
 celery soup
1 cup 2% milk
½ teaspoon garlic powder
½ teaspoon paprika
¼ teaspoon dried basil
½ teaspoon salt
½ teaspoon black pepper
2 (6-ounce) cans tuna, drained
1 cup shredded Cheddar cheese
½ cup crushed potato chips
 (optional)

Directions.

1. Preheat oven to 350°F.

2. Combine noodles, soup, milk, garlic powder, paprika, basil, salt, and pepper, and stir. Fold in tuna.

3. Spoon into sprayed 11x7-inch casserole dish. Top with cheese. Cover and bake until bubbly, about 35 minutes. Sprinkle potato chips on top if desired.

Makes 6 servings.

LOADED BAKED POTATO SOUP

A loaded baked potato in creamy soup form? Yes, please! Take the time to cook the potatoes in the oven for this recipe, which will give the soup a richer, more complex flavor.

Ingredients

3 medium white potatoes
6 slices bacon
1 tablespoon unsalted butter
1 large white onion, finely chopped
1 tablespoon all-purpose flour
1 (14.5-ounce) can chicken broth
1 teaspoon garlic powder
3 cups 2% milk
1 teaspoon salt
1 teaspoon black pepper
1 cup shredded cheddar cheese
¼ cup chopped scallions or basil for garnish

Directions

1. Preheat oven to 400°F. Bake potatoes 1 hour or until tender when pierced.

2. When cool enough to handle, peel potatoes. Mash two-thirds of potatoes with potato masher. Chop remaning third into bite-sized pieces. Set aside.

3. Place bacon in large skillet, then heat to medium-low. Cook, flipping once, until cooked through and edges start to curl, about 8–12 minutes. Remove bacon to paper towels to drain. Crumble when cool. Set aside.

4. In large pot over medium-low heat, melt butter. Raise heat to medium-high and add onion, stirring occasionally, until tender, about 3–5 minutes. Remove from heat and stir in flour. Add broth, garlic powder, milk, salt, and pepper. Bring mixture to a simmer over medium heat, stirring occasionally, about 5 minutes, until soup has thickened slightly.

5. Add mashed potatoes and cook 1 minute more. Do not allow soup to boil.

Gently stir in remaining potatoes. Sprinkle each serving with bacon and cheese. Garnish with scallions or basil.

Makes 4 servings.

FRENCH-QUARTER ONION SOUP

If I'm at a restaurant that offers French onion soup, I always want to order it. This version uses fontina cheese, which all the best restaurants use, and features a creamy broth in the New Orleans style.

Ingredients

6 tablespoons unsalted butter, divided
2 large Vidalia onions, sliced
3 medium red onions, sliced
2 (32-ounce) cartons beef broth
1 teaspoon garlic powder
1 bay leaf
¼ teaspoon ground thyme
½ cup heavy cream
½ teaspoon salt
½ teaspoon black pepper
1 cup shredded fontina cheese
Country bread, for serving

Directions

1. In large pot over medium-low heat, melt 4 tablespoons butter. Add onions and cook, stirring occasionally to scrape up browned bits, until soft and brown, about 30 minutes. Lower heat if needed to not burn onions.

2. Add ¼ cup broth to pot, scraping with wooden spoon to

release brown bits, then add rest of broth, garlic powder, bay leaf, and thyme.

3. Raise heat to bring mixture just to the boil, lower heat, and simmer another 20 minutes.

4. Remove bay leaf. Add soup to blender in batches and puree until smooth. Stir in cream, salt, and pepper and transfer soup to oven-safe bowls.

5. Preheat broiler. Cut country

bread in rounds and butter with remaining butter. Place slices on baking sheet and place under broiler until butter is melted and bread is crispy, about 1 minute.

6. Top each bowl with toasted bread and fontina cheese, and place bowls on baking sheet under broiler, about 1–2 minutes, or until cheese is golden brown.

Makes 6–8 servings.

MIDWESTERN MOSTACHOLI

In many parts of the United States you might call this dish "baked ziti," but in the Midwest, we have mostacholi. Mostacholi noodles are just like ziti noodles except they usually have lines; use a large penne or ziti if you can't find them at your supermarket.

Instructions

½ of 1 (16-ounce) package mostacholi noodles, cooked
1 cup ricotta cheese
1 large egg, beaten
¼ teaspoon dried oregano
¼ teaspoon garlic powder
½ teaspoon salt
¼ teaspoon black pepper
1 cup shredded mozzarella, divided
½ cup grated Parmesan cheese
1 (24- to 26-ounce) jar marinara sauce with meat (about 3½ cups)

Directions

1. Preheat oven to 450°F.

2. In small bowl, combine ricotta, egg, oregano, garlic powder, salt, pepper, and half of mozzarella. Set aside.

3. In bottom of 11x7-inch casserole dish, spread half of marinara sauce.

Top with mostacholi, then ricotta mixture and remaining sauce. Sprinkle with ½ cup Parmesan and remaining mozzarella. Bake until top is browned and sauce is bubbling, 25–30 minutes.

Makes 3–4 servings.

ROASTED VEGETABLE CASEROLE

In my house, you can get away with a vegetable dish as a main – as long as it has some bacon thrown in. This casserole is perfect for summer, when you sometimes want a lighter meal for dinner.

Ingredients
4 slices bacon
1 medium yellow onion
4 medium summer squash, sliced
 about ⅛-inch thick
¼ cup plus 1 teaspoon salt,
 divided
2 large eggs
1 tablespoon mayonnaise
1½ cups shredded cheddar cheese
½ teaspoon garlic powder
¼ teaspoon basil
¾ teaspoon black pepper

1 pint grape or cherry tomatoes,
 halved or quartered

Directions
1. Preheat oven to 350°F.

2. Grate onion with box grater and set aside.

3. Toss squash with ¼ cup salt, then place in colander to drain for at least 15 minutes. Rinse off excess salt, then pat dry with paper towels.

4. Place bacon in large skillet, then heat to medium-low. Cook, flipping once, until cooked through and edges start to curl, about 8–12 minutes. Remove bacon to paper towels to drain. Crumble when cool.

5. In medium bowl, combine bacon, onion, eggs, mayonnaise, cheddar cheese, garlic powder, basil, remaining 1 teaspoon salt, and pepper.

6. In lightly greased 11x7-inch casserole dish, spread half of sliced squash across bottom of pan, then top with ½ of tomatoes and half of cheese mixture. Repeat with another layer.

7. Bake covered, for about 45 minutes; uncover and continue to bake for 15 minutes, or until vegetables are tender and cooked through and cheese is bubbly.

Makes 4 servings.

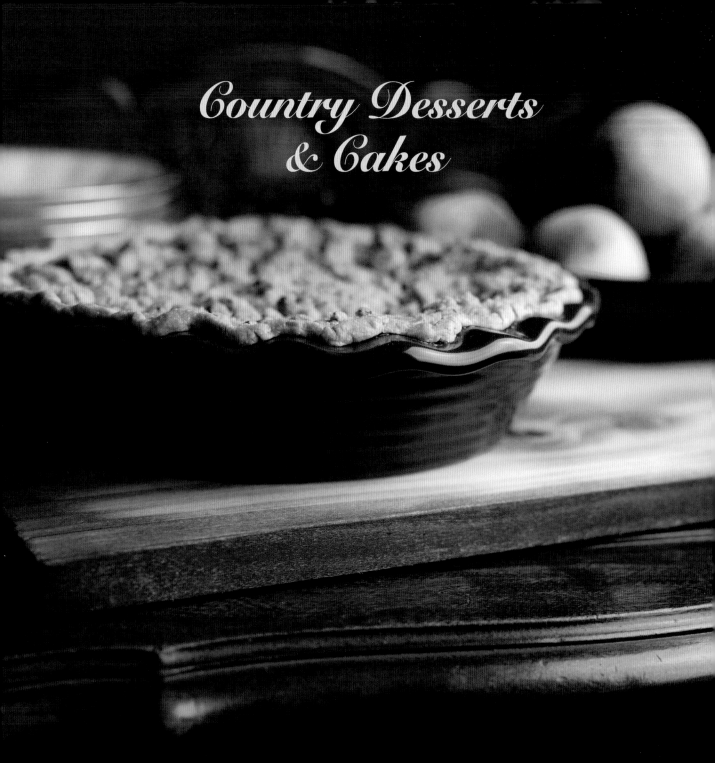

Country Desserts & Cakes

COCONUT CREAM PIE

Coconut cream pie is the perfect light and fluffy palate cleanser after a big country meal. This version also couldn't be easier — just make sure to leave enough time for it to firm up in the refrigerator.

Ingredients

1 (6-ounce) ready-to-fill 9-inch
 piecrust
2 (3.4-ounce) packages coconut
cream–flavor instant pudding and
 pie filling
2 cups cold milk
2 cups frozen whipped topping,
 thawed and divided
¾ cup sweetened flaked coconut,
 plus 2–3 tablespoons for topping

Directions

1. Place crust in 9-inch pie plate, and bake according to package instructions.

2. In large bowl, whisk together pudding mix and milk for 2 minutes. Stir in 1 cup whipped topping and ¾ cup coconut; pour into crust. Refrigerate 4 hours or until firm.

3. Meanwhile, in small skillet over medium heat, toast remaining coconut until golden brown. Remove from heat and set aside.

4. Top pie with remaining whipped topping and sprinkle with toasted coconut.

Makes 6–8 servings.

GRANDMA'S BUTTERSCOTCH PIE

When I was a kid, I never knew how easy butterscotch was to make in your kitchen, so I always thought my grandmother was a baking genius when she made this sweet pie, which was handed down from her mother.

Ingredients
Pie
1 refrigerated piecrust
2 tablespoons unsalted butter
3 tablespoons all-purpose flour
1¼ cups light brown sugar
2¼ cups 2% milk
⅛ teaspoon salt
3 large eggs yolks, beaten
1½ teaspoons vanilla extract

Meringue
3 large egg whites
¼ teaspoon cream of tartar
½ cup sugar
Caramel pieces, for garnish
 (optional)

Directions
Pie
1. Bake piecrust according to package directions. Then set oven temperature to 350°F.

2. In medium saucepan, melt butter. Remove from heat, add flour, and whisk until smooth. Stir in brown sugar. Return to heat; whisk in milk and salt until blended. Cook and whisk over medium-high heat until thickened and bubbly. Reduce heat; cook and stir 2 minutes longer. Remove from heat.

3. In small bowl, combine 1 cup hot filling with egg yolks and mix well to combine. Return all to pan, stirring constantly. Bring mixture to a gentle boil; cook and stir for 2 minutes longer. Remove from heat and gently stir in vanilla. Pour mixture into piecrust.

Meringue
1. In small bowl, beat egg whites and cream of tartar with hand mixer on medium speed until soft peaks form. Gradually beat in sugar, about 1 tablespoon at a time, on high until stiff glossy peaks form and sugar is dissolved. Spread evenly over hot filling.

2. Bake pie for 12–15 minutes or until meringue is slightly browned. Cool on wire rack for 1 hour, then refrigerate for at least 3 hours before serving. Top with caramel pieces if desired.

Makes 6–8 servings.

FRENCH SILK PIE WITH COOKIE CRUMBLES

Anyone who grew up in the Midwest east of the Mississippi can remember peering into the kids'-eye-level pie case at the front of Bakers Square restaurant (formerly called Poppin' Fresh Pies). My eyes were always on the French Silk! These days I prefer mine with cookie crumbles, but to keep it authentic you can use a vegetable peeler to peel off some chocolate curls, too.

Ingredients

1 refrigerated piecrust, at room temperature
6 ounces unsweetened baking chocolate, chopped
1 (14-ounce) can sweetened condensed milk
½ teaspoon vanilla extract
1 (8-ounce) container frozen whipped topping, thawed and divided
3 crunchy chocolate-chip cookies, crumbled

Directions

1. Heat oven to 425°F. Place piecrust in 9-inch glass pie plate. Line piecrust with foil; pierce bottom with holes to let out steam.

2. Bake 8 minutes. Remove foil; bake 5–7 minutes longer or until golden brown. Cool completely, about 20 minutes.

3. Meanwhile, in large microwavable bowl, microwave chocolate on high 1–1½ minutes, stirring every 30 seconds, until melted and smooth. Stir in condensed milk and vanilla and whisk until smooth; let stand 2 minutes. Fold half of whipped topping into chocolate mixture until blended; pour mixture into crust.

4. Cover and refrigerate 4-8 hours or until firm. Spread remaining whipped topping over pie; garnish with crushed cookies.

Makes 6–8 servings.

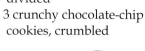

ICEBOX LEMON PIE

If you like your desserts tart and tangy you'll love this no-bake lemon pie. After refrigerating you can keep it covered in the freezer for a week or more, so it's perfect for when you have to bring a dessert to an event and know you'll be pressed for time beforehand.

Ingredients
1 (6-ounce) graham-cracker
  piecrust
1 (8-ounce) package cream cheese,
  softened
1 (14-ounce) can sweetened
  condensed milk
½ cup freshly squeezed lemon
  juice
Zest from 1 lemon (about 1
  tablespoon)
1–2 tablespoons powdered sugar

Directions
1. Place piecrust in 9-inch pie plate.

2. In large bowl, beat all ingredients except powdered sugar until smooth. Spread mixture evenly in crust. Refrigerate at least 4 hours and up to 8 hours.

3. Sprinkle powdered sugar on top before serving.

Makes 6–8 servings.

STRAWBERRY-RHUBARB PIE

When I think of the quintessential country dessert, I think of strawberry-rhubarb pie — and in my mind, it always has a lattice top. Lattices are much easier than you'd think, especially for how impressive they look. Simply take a round of piecrust and slice it into strips with a pizza cutter before placing on top of the pie.

Ingredients
2 refrigerated piecrusts, chilled
2½ cups strawberries, hulled and chopped
2½ cups red rhubarb, chopped
1 cup sugar
⅓ cup all-purpose flour
1 teaspoon lemon juice
½ teaspoon vanilla extract
2 tablespoons cold unsalted butter, cut into ¼-inch pieces
1 large egg yolk
1 teaspoon water

Directions
1. Preheat oven to 450°F.

2. Transfer 1 piecrust to 9-inch pie dish. Trim excess dough, leaving ¾-inch overhang. Poke bottom of piecrust in several places with tines of a fork. Roll out remaining piecrust and slice into ½-inch strips.

3. Mix strawberries, rhubarb, sugar, flour, lemon juice, and vanilla. Pour fruit mixture into piecrust. Dot with butter pieces.

4. Moisten edge of bottom crust with a finger dipped in water. Lay 7 dough strips across top of filling, then form a lattice pattern by placing remaining dough strips in opposite direction. Trim ends of dough strips even with overhang of bottom crust. Fold strip ends and overhang under, pressing to seal. Crimp edges.

5. Beat together egg and water and brush over crust. Transfer pie plate to a baking sheet.

6. Bake for 15 minutes, then reduce heat to 350°F and bake another 30 minutes, or until crust is golden brown and filling is bubbling.

7. Remove from oven and cool on rack before serving.

Makes 6–8 servings.

OLD-FASHONED APPLE PIE

Whoever coined the phrase "easy as pie" never tried to make an apple pie that didn't have a soggy bottom. But this pie recipe is no-fail: Freezing the dough first in the pie plate makes sure it doesn't heat up too fast, and cooking the apples before you add them to the pie reduces the amount of moisture they contain.

Ingredients

2 tablespoons unsalted butter
7–8 medium baking apples (such as Granny Smith or Honeycrisp), peeled, cored, and cut into wedges
½ teaspoon ground cinnamon
¼ teaspoon ground nutmeg
¼ teaspoon salt
¾ cup plus 2 tablespoons sugar, divided
2 tablespoons all-purpose flour
2 teaspoons cornstarch
2 teaspoons apple cider vinegar
2 refrigerated piecrusts, thawed
1 large egg, beaten

Directions

1. Preheat oven to 425°F and place large baking sheet on middle oven rack.

2. In large skillet over medium-high heat, melt butter and add apples to pan. Stir to coat fruit with butter and cook, stirring occasionally, until apples are almost tender, 6–7 minutes.

3. Meanwhile, whisk together spices, salt, and ¾ cup sugar, and sprinkle over skillet, stirring to combine. Lower heat and cook until apples have started to soften, approximately 5–7 minutes.

4. Sprinkle flour and cornstarch over apples and continue to cook, stirring occasionally, another 3–5 minutes. Remove pan from heat, stir in vinegar, then scrape fruit mixture into bowl and allow to cool completely. (The fruit mixture will cool faster if spread out on a rimmed baking sheet.)

5. Press crust into 9-inch pie plate, trimming to leave ½-inch overhang. Place plate, with dough, in freezer for 10 minutes.

6. Remove piecrust from freezer and put cooled pie filling into it. Cover with remaining dough. Press edges together, trim excess, then crimp edges with tines of a fork. Using a sharp knife, cut 5 steam vents in top of crust. Lightly brush top of pie with egg and sprinkle with remaining sugar.

7. Place pie in oven and bake on hot baking sheet for 20 minutes, then reduce temperature to 375°F. Continue to cook until interior is bubbling and crust is golden brown, about 30–40 minutes more. Remove and allow to cool on kitchen rack, about 2 hours.

Makes 6–8 servings.

CINNAMON-APPLE CRUMBLE

Apple pie is a must-have at certain holidays, but I've always loved apple crumble more. It's sweet, yet tangy, soft, yet crisp . . . but that crumble! You can't beat the topping on an apple crumble. Pair it with some vanilla ice cream for an even more indulgent treat.

Ingredients
4 medium baking apples (such as
 Granny Smith or Honeycrisp),
 peeled, cored, and chopped
1 teaspoon lemon juice
½ cup water
1 teaspoon cinnamon
¼ teaspoon allspice
¾ cup all-purpose flour
1 cup sugar
⅓ cup salted butter

Directions
1. Preheat oven to 350°F.

2. In large bowl, mix together apples, lemon juice, water, cinnamon, and allspice. Pour into lightly greased 13x9-inch casserole dish.

3. In medium bowl, mash together flour, sugar, and butter until crumbly. Spread over apple mixture.

4. Bake, uncovered, until apples are tender, about 30 minutes.

Makes 6–8 servings.

JUST PEACHY COBBLER

My Midwestern grandmother may have been the queen of fruit pies, making several for every holiday, but she couldn't top my Southern grandmother's peach cobbler, and with good reason! Her delicious secret was using canned peaches and reserving some of the syrup to use as a sweetener.

Ingredients
2 (14.5-ounce) cans sliced peaches in syrup
½ cup unsalted butter, melted
1 cup all-purpose flour
1 cup sugar
1½ teaspoons baking powder
¼ teaspoon salt
1 cup 2% milk
Whipped cream, for garnish

Directions
1. Preheat oven to 350°F.

2. Drain 1 can of peaches; reserve syrup from the other. Spread melted butter in 2-quart baking dish.

3. In medium bowl, mix flour, sugar, baking powder, and salt. Stir in milk and reserved syrup.

4. Pour batter over melted butter in baking dish. Arrange peaches over batter. Bake for 1 hour or until batter rises around peaches and crust is thick and golden brown. Serve warm with whipped cream.

Makes 6 servings.

OATMEAL-PLUM POUND CAKE

Every time fall rolls around I want to make this pound cake, which reminds me of the delicious holiday cooking in the months to come. Make it for dessert but save some for breakfast the next day.

Ingredients

2 cups all-purpose flour
⅓ cup light brown sugar
2½ teaspoons baking powder
¾ teaspoon baking soda
½ teaspoon salt
1 cup quick-cooking oats (not instant)
1 cup chopped, pitted firm-ripe plums (about 2)
½ teaspoon cinnamon
1 large egg, lightly beaten
1 cup buttermilk
2 tablespoons vegetable oil

Directions

1. Preheat oven to 350°F.

2. In large bowl, combine flour, brown sugar, baking powder, baking soda, and salt. Stir in oats, plums, and walnuts.

3. In small bowl, whisk together egg, buttermilk, and oil. Pour all at once into dry ingredients. Stir just until lumps start to disappear. Turn into lightly greased 9x5 loaf pan.

4. Bake for 45 minutes or until toothpick inserted in center comes out clean. Remove loaf from pan to wire rack to cool. Store overnight for easier slicing.

Makes 8 servings.

CLASSIC COLA CAKE

Chocolate joins with its fizzy cousin in this delicious dessert that uses cola in the sauce and in the cake batter itself. If you're in a hurry, just buy a box of chocolate cake mix and prepare as directed on box, substituting cola for water.

Ingredients
Cake
1 cup sugar
1 cup all-purpose flour
½ stick unsalted butter, melted
¼ cup vegetable oil
1 cup cola
¼ cup 2% milk
½ teaspoon baking soda
1½ tablespoons unsweetened
  cocoa powder
1 large egg

Chocolate-Cola Sauce
1 cup cola
½ cup sugar

¾ cup unsweetened cocoa powder
⅓ cup semisweet chocolate chips,
  finely chopped

Directions
Cake
1. Heat oven to 325°F; grease two 8-inch round cake pans.

2. In large bowl, mix together sugar and flour.

3. In small saucepan, combine melted butter, oil, and cola; bring to a boil. Slowly add cola mixture to flour blend. Whisk to combine well.

4. Add milk and baking soda; mix well. Stir in cocoa powder and egg, whisking well after each addition.

5. Pour batter into prepared pan and bake until toothpick inserted into the center comes out clean, about 30 minutes. Let cake cool before removing from pan.

Chocolate-Cola Sauce
1. In medium saucepan, whisk together cola, sugar, and cocoa powder.

2. Heat mixture over medium heat, whisking frequently. Once it just begins to boil, remove

from heat and stir in chopped chocolate until melted. Pour sauce over cake.

Makes 8 servings.

MISSISSIPPI MUD CAKE

Even though "Mississippi" is in its name, this cake is popular in many states and has lots of different variations. Most contain marshmallows and pecans, but this one has a crispy, crunchy twist: puffed-rice cereal mixed into the chocolate on top.

Ingredients
Cake
2 cups all-purpose flour
2 cups sugar
¼ teaspoon salt
½ cup unsalted butter
½ cup vegetable oil
½ cup unsweetened cocoa powder
¼ cup water
2 large eggs
1 teaspoon baking soda
½ cup 2% milk
2 teaspoons vanilla extract
1 (10.5-ounce) bag miniature marshmallows

Topping
½ cup unsalted butter, softened
3 tablespoons unsweetened cocoa powder
6 tablespoons 2% milk
1 (16-ounce) package powdered sugar
1 cup chopped pecans
1½ cups puffed rice cereal

Directions
Cake
1. Preheat oven to 350°F.

2. In large bowl, combine flour, sugar, and salt. Set aside.

3. In small saucepan, bring butter, oil, cocoa powder, and water to a boil. Stir into to the flour mixture until combined.

4. In small bowl, whisk together eggs, baking soda, milk, and vanilla until well-blended. Add to flour mixture, mix well, and pour into lightly greased 13x9-inch casserole dish. Bake until toothpick inserted in the center comes out clean, about 25–30 minutes. Allow to cool slightly, then cover top with marshmallows.

Topping
1. In small saucepan, melt butter over low heat. Add cocoa powder

and milk and stir well to combine. Heat, stirring constantly, until mixture starts to bubble. Remove from heat. Stir in powdered sugar. Slowly mix in nuts and cereal.

2. Pour warm icing over cake and marshmallows. Cool before serving.

Makes 12–14 servings.

APPLE UPSIDE-DOWN CAKE

This classy take on a pineapple upside-down cake looks even better if you take a little time to nicely arrange the apples on the bottom.

Ingredients
1½ cups all-purpose flour
1½ teaspoons baking powder
½ teaspoon ground cinnamon
½ teaspoon salt
½ cup unsalted butter, softened, plus more for coating pan
½ cup granulated sugar
½ cup 2% or whole milk
2 large eggs
1 teaspoon vanilla extract
½ cup light brown sugar
3 firm baking apples (such as Braeburn, Fuji, or Honeycrisp), cored and sliced
1 tablespoon apple cider vinegar

Directions
1. Preheat oven to 350°F.

2. In medium bowl, mix together flour, baking powder, cinnamon, and salt. Set aside.

3. In large bowl, beat butter and granulated sugar with an electric mixer on high, until light and fluffy. Add milk, eggs, and vanilla, and beat until incorporated.

4. Set mixer on low, then add flour mixture in batches until incorporated.

5. Grease 9-inch round cake pan generously with butter; sprinkle bottom with brown sugar. Toss apples with vinegar and arrange in overlapping circles until bottom is covered (some apple slices may remain). Spoon batter over apples.

6. Bake until toothpick inserted in center comes out clean, about 45–50 minutes. Cool cake in pan on wire rack, at least 30 minutes. Before serving, release cake from pan by running a knife around the edge, then carefully turn over onto a platter.

Makes 8–12 servings.

SOUTHERN PECAN CHEESCAKE

It wasn't long after American cream cheese was invented that the cheesecake was born, based off of a European pastry that was baked with French cheese. This version uses pecans (the most Southern of all nuts) in both the batter and as a decorative and delicious crust.

Ingredients
1½ cups graham cracker crumbs
1 cup plus 3 tablespoons sugar, divided
½ teaspoon cinnamon
⅓ cup unsalted butter, melted
4 (8-ounce) packages cream cheese, softened
½ cup sour cream
1 teaspoon vanilla
4 large eggs
1½ cups pecans, divided

Directions
1. Preheat oven to 325°F.

2. In medium bowl, mix together graham cracker crumbs, 3 tablespoons sugar, cinnamon, and butter; press onto bottom of 9-inch springform pan.

3. In large bowl, beat cream cheese, sour cream, remaining sugar, and vanilla with mixer until blended. Add eggs, 1 at a time, mixing on low speed after each just until blended. Fold in ¾ cup pecans. Pour over crust.

4. Bake 55 minutes or until center is almost set. Run knife around rim of pan to loosen cake; cool completely before removing rim. Refrigerate cheesecake 4 hours. Crush remaining pecans and press into sides of cheesecake.

Makes 8 servings.

PUMPKIN SPICE PIE

Perfect or bringing along when you have Thanksgiving at someone else's home, this pie is also great for leftovers! There's nothing better than enjoying a pumpkin spice latté in the morning with a slice of this pie next to it.

Ingredients

Pastry

1¼ cups all-purpose flour
Pinch of salt
½ cup butter or margarine
About 2 tbsp cold water

Filling

3 eggs, separated
2 cups canned pumpkin purée
½ cup plus 2 tablespoons sugar
1 cup sour cream
1 teaspoon cinnamon
¼ teaspoon ground ginger
¼ teaspoon ground nutmeg
¼ teaspoon ground cloves
¼ teaspoon salt

Garnish

⅔ cup whipped cream
1 teaspoon nutmeg for dusting

Direction

1. Place the flour and salt in a bowl, add the butter or margarine and rub it into the flour until it resembles fine breadcrumbs. Add the water and knead the mixture into a ball. Cover with plastic wrap and refrigerate for 1 hour.

2. Preheat the oven to 400°F. Roll out the pastry and use it to line a 9-inch cake pan.

3. Whisk the egg whites until they form soft peaks. Beat together the egg yolks, pumpkin, sugar, sour cream, spices and salt until blended, then fold in the egg whites. Spoon the mixture into the pastry shell and bake for 10 minutes. Reduce the temperature to 350°F and continue to bake for about 30 minutes or until the filling is just set and the crust golden brown.

4. Remove from the oven and leave to cool, then refrigerate until required. Remove the pie from the pan, place on a serving dish, then pipe the top with a circle of cream and dust with nutmeg.

Makes 6–8 servings.

STRAWBERRY SHORTCAKE TRIFLE

There's nothing classier at the end of a dinner party than a layered dessert in individual parfait glasses. (If you have a large trifle bowl, you can use that too.) This recipe mixes fresh strawberries with frozen ones to give them the perfect amount of sweetness. It saves money, too!

Ingredients

2 (1-pint) cartons fresh
   strawberries, divided
1 (14-ounce) package frozen sliced
   strawberries in syrup, thawed
2 tablespoons lemon juice
3 cups vanilla yogurt
1 (3.4-ounce) package cheesecake
   instant pudding and pie filling
1 (8-ounce) container frozen
   whipped topping, thawed and
   divided
1 (10.75-ounce) frozen pound cake,
   thawed and chopped into 1-inch
   cubes
Powdered sugar, for serving

Directions

1. Set aside 8–10 fresh strawberries for garnishes, then hull and slice remaining strawberries.

2. In medium bowl, combine fresh strawberries and (thawed) frozen strawberries in syrup. Mix well.

3. In separate medium bowl, whisk lemon juice, yogurt, and pudding mix until smooth; fold in 1 cup whipped topping.

4. To assemble trifle, place pound cake cubes into bottom of trifle glasses. Top with half of strawberry mixture, then half of yogurt mixture. Repeat layers and top with strawberry garnish. Dust with powdered sugar before serving.

Makes 8–10 servings.

SWEET BUTTER CUPCAKES

Butter makes everything better! In these cupcakes, it makes both a rich and fluffy cake and a light and airy buttercream frosting. Save the chocolate for another time and give these out to vanilla-lovers.

Ingredients
Cupcakes
3 cups all-purpose flour
¾ teaspoon baking powder
¼ teaspoon salt
1½ cups unsalted butter, softened
2½ cups granulated sugar
5 large eggs
2 teaspoons vanilla extract
1 cup 2% or whole milk

Frosting
3 cups powdered sugar
⅓ cup salted butter, softened
1½ teaspoons vanilla
1–2 tablespoons 2% milk

Directions
Cupcakes
1. Preheat oven to 350°F.

2. In medium bowl, combine flour, baking powder, and salt. Set aside.

3. In large bowl with electric mixer, cream butter and sugar on medium until light and fluffy, about 2 minutes. Add eggs one at a time, mixing well after each addition. Mix in vanilla.

3. Add flour mixture to sugar mixture alternately with milk, starting with the flour.
Pour into 2 lightly greased 12-cup muffin tins (or use cupcake liners) and bake 20–25 minutes or until toothpick inserted comes out clean. Cool 10 minutes in pan on rack; remove and cool completely before decorating with frosting.

Frosting
1. In medium bowl, mix powdered sugar and butter with electric mixer on low speed. Stir in vanilla and 1 tablespoon of milk.

2. Gradually beat in just enough remaining milk to make frosting smooth and spreadable. Spread on cooled cupcakes.

Makes 24 cupcakes.

CANDY BAR CUPCAKES

These cupcakes filled with melted candy bars are a hit with kids and adults alike. If making them for kids, keep them simple – you may even want to buy store-bought frosting (trust me, they won't notice). If they're for an adult party crowd, fancy them up by adding mini-chocolate chips and a drizzle of caramel sundae stopping.

Ingredients
Cupcakes
¾ cup unsalted butter, softened
¾ cup granulated sugar
½ cup light brown sugar
3 large eggs
2 cups all-purpose flour
2 teaspoons baking powder
¼ teaspoon salt
¾ cup 2% or whole milk
1 teaspoon vanilla extract
12 mini candy bars, or 6 "fun-sized" candy bars, halved, plus more for garnish

Peanut Butter Frosting
½ cup unsalted butter, softened
1 cup creamy peanut butter
2 cups powdered sugar
3 tablespoons 2% milk, or as needed
Caramel sundae topping, for garnish (optional)
Mini chocolate chips, for garnish (optional)

Directions
Cupcakes
1. Preheat oven to 350°F. Place cupcake liners in 12-cup muffin tin.

2. In large bowl, beat together butter and sugars until light and fluffy. Beat in eggs, one at a time, until fully combined.

3. In medium bowl, whisk together dry ingredients. In liquid measuring cup, mix together milk and vanilla and set aside.

4. Add ⅓ of flour mixture to sugar mixture and stir to combine, then add ½ of milk. Alternate with remaining flour and milk, ending with flour.

5. Evenly divide batter among cupcake liners. Press one piece of candy in center of each cupcake. Bake 12–14 minutes or until light golden on top. Remove from oven and allow to cool on a wire rack.

Peanut Butter Frosting
1. In medium bowl, mix together butter and peanut butter with electric mixer. Gradually mix in sugar and incorporate milk, 1 tablespoon at a time, until all sugar is mixed in and frosting is thick, fluffy, and spreadable, at least 3 minutes.

2. Decorate cupcakes with frosting and garnish with candy and other garnishes, if desired.

Makes 12 cupcakes.

OLD-FASHIONED CHOCOLATE CHIP COOKIES

As I've adapted my grandparents' recipes for my own tastes, one ingredient I often find myself taking out is vegetable shortening. For this cookie recipe, however, the shortening is completely necessary to give the cookies their perfect texture.

Ingredients

2½ cups all-purpose flour
1 teaspoon baking soda
1 teaspoon salt
½ cup vegetable shortening
½ cup unsalted butter, softened
1½ cups light brown sugar
2 teaspoons vanilla
2 large eggs
1 (12-ounce) package semisweet chocolate chips

Directions

1. Preheat oven to 375°F.

2. In medium bowl, mix flour, baking soda, and salt.

3. In large bowl, beat shortening and butter until creamy. Add sugar and vanilla and beat with mixer on medium speed until well blended. Beat in eggs, one at a time, mixing well between each addition.

4. Add flour mixture to sugar mixture, and beat slowly to incorporate, then beat to blend well. Stir in chocolate chips.

5. Drop batter in 2-tablespoon portions about 2 inches apart on ungreased baking sheet.
Bake about 10 minutes or until edges of cookies are brown. Let cookies cool on baking sheet about

5 minutes, then transfer to racks with a spatula. Serve warm or cool.

Makes about 36 cookies.

FARM-STAND WHOOPIE PIES

Whoopie pies (which aren't actually pies at all) were originally made by the wives of Amish farmers in Pennsylvania, who were said to yell "whoopie!" when they found them in their packed lunches. Anyone you make these handheld desserts for is sure to be equally as thrilled.

Ingredients

3 cups sugar
1 cup unsalted butter
4 large eggs
½ cup vegetable oil
2 teaspoons vanilla extract
6 cups all-purpose flour
2 cups unsweetened cocoa powder
1½ tablespoons baking soda
1 teaspoon baking powder
1 teaspoon salt
3 cups 2% milk
1 (12-ounce) carton whipped-style frosting

Directions

1. Preheat oven to 350°F.

2. In large bowl, beat sugar, butter, and eggs together with an electric mixer on medium until well combined, about 3 minutes. Add oil and vanilla and beat again for 1 minute.

3. In separate large bowl, combine all dry ingredients. Add half of dry mixture to sugar mixture and beat until blended. Add half of milk, then remaining dry mixture, then remaining milk, fully incorporating each addition.

4. With ice cream scoop or serving spoon, scoop out 32 circles of batter onto lightly greased baking sheets. Bake for 10–12 minutes or until toothpick inserted in center comes out clean. Let cool.

5. Spread frosting onto 16 circles and place remaining circles on top to form whoopie pies.

Makes 16 whoopie pies.

MELT-IN-YOUR-MOUTH FRITTERS WITH FRUIT DIPS

These mouthfuls of sweet batter are deep-fried until delicately crisp, then served with two tangy fruit sauces. Eat them while they are still hot and as light as a feather.

Ingredients

8 oz raspberries
4 tablespoons superfine sugar
Small can of apricots in juice
9 level tablespoons all-purpose flour
Pinch of salt
4 tablespoons butter
3 large eggs
½ teaspoon each nutmeg and cinnamon
Oil for deep-frying
Confectioners' sugar

Directions

1. Cook the raspberries with sugar to taste until soft, then sieve out all the seeds. Chill until required.

2. Blend the apricots with sufficient juice to give a smooth pouring sauce, then stir in the rum. Chill until required.

3. Sift the flour and salt onto a sheet of waxed paper.

4. Melt the butter with ³/₄ cup of water and bring to a rolling boil. Remove from the heat and pour in the flour and salt mixture all at once, then beat quickly to a stiff paste. Continue cooking and beating until the mixture comes clean away from the sides of the pan. Don't overbeat or the dough will become tough. Cool slightly.

5. Beat the eggs together, then gradually beat sufficient egg into the paste to produce a smooth and glossy batter. Add the nutmeg and cinnamon, mixing them well in. (The batter should be of a fairly soft, dropping consistency.)

6. When ready to cook, heat the oil in a deep-fryer to 350°F. Drop small spoonfuls of batter carefully into the oil, and don't cook too many at a time. Cook for about 1 minute, removing the fritters when golden all over and drain on paper towels. Keep warm while you cook the rest.

7. Top the fritters with a little sieved confectioners' sugar before serving with both sauces, either warm or chilled.

Makes 4 servings

DIVINE PECAN CAKE

This is very, very rich! However, a little spice can be added which will help balance the sweetness.

Ingredients
Cake
1½ cups pecan halves
3 cups all-purpose flour
1½ teaspoons salt
1 tablespoon ground cinnamon
1 tablespoon ground nutmeg
1 cup unsalted butter
1½ cups superfine sugar
5 eggs
1 tsp vanilla extract
2 tablespoons milk

Frosting
3 cups confectioners' sugar
3 egg whites, at room temperature
3–4 tablespoons chocolate-nut spread

Directions
1. Set aside about 10 pecan halves for decoration. Meanwhile, place the remainder on an oven tray and roast at 350°F for about 10 minutes, then whizz in a food processor, taking care not to chop the nuts too finely.

2. Grease, flour or line two or four 8-inch matching cake pans. Sift the dry ingredients together into a large bowl.

3. Cream the butter and sugar until pale and fluffy, then beat in the eggs, one at a time, adding a little flour to prevent separation. Blend in the rest of the flour mixture, the chopped nuts, vanilla, and sufficient milk to give a soft dropping consistency.

4. Divide the mixture evenly among the pans and bake for about 30 minutes if using two pans, 20–25 minutes if using four. When the cakes are just firm to the touch, leave to cool in the oven, then turn them out onto a tray or large board until completely cold.

5. Place the sifted confectioners' sugar and egg whites in a large mixing bowl over a pan of simmering water. Whisk, gradually increasing speed, until the mixture becomes thick, glossy and stands up in peaks.

6. If 2 pans have been used, cut the cakes to make 4 layers. Place the base layer on a board or serving plate, then stack up the others, covering the first and third layers with frosting, and using chocolate-nut spread on the middle layer. When all four layers are assembled, spread the sides and top with the rest of the white frosting and decorate with the reserved pecan halves.

Tip: If you have only two pans and need to split the cakes, be sure to chill them well before attempting to slice them horizontally.

Makes 10–12 servings.

PECAN PIE

This is an irresistible Southern classic, originating from the early days of pecan growing in Louisiana. Serve with whipped cream or vanilla ice cream.

Ingredients

9-inch pre-baked pie crust (can be bought)
½ cup superfine sugar
Scant cup light brown sugar
¾ cup butter, melted
4 very large eggs
1 teaspoon vanilla extract
1 cup pecan nuts, chopped
1-2 cups pecan halves
Superfine sugar for sprinkling

Directions

1. Place the pie shell on a cookie sheet. Preheat the oven to 400°F.

2. Melt the two sugars and the butter slowly in a pan until the sugar dissolves. Cool slightly. Beat the eggs in a large bowl, then beat in the sugar-butter mixture and the vanilla extract.

3. Stir in the chopped nuts and pour carefully into the pie shell. Bake for 15–20 minutes, then arrange the halved nuts neatly on the top. Bake for a further 20 minutes or until the filling is firm to the touch.

Makes 8 servings.

KEY LIME PIE

If you decide to use actual Key limes you will find that, though flavorful, they are quite small and you will need three times as many to yield the amount of juice you require. This recipe uses regular limes.

Ingredients
Crumb crust
1 graham-cracker piecrust

Filling
Finely grated rind and juice of
 4 limes
15-oz can sweetened condensed
 milk
1 envelope (2¼ teaspoons)
 powdered gelatin
1¼ cups whipped cream

Directions
1. Place piecrust in 9-inch pie plate

2. Mix together the grated rind and juice and the condensed milk, then chill.

3. Place the gelatin in a small bowl and pour on 2–3 tablespoons of very hot (not boiling) water. Stir until blended then microwave on full power in 15–20-second bursts, or place the bowl over a small pan of boiling water until the gelatin becomes quite clear. Stir into the milk mixture and mix thoroughly.

4. Fold the whipped cream into the lime filling. When lightly blended, spoon into the crumb crust and level the top. Chill for 3 hours until firm.

5. To serve, carefully transfer the pie from the pan to a serving dish. Pipe swirls of whipped cream around the edge and decorate with lime slices.

Makes 8 servings.

BLUEBERRY PIE

Pies came to America with the Pilgrims and we have been having a love affair with them since. Ice cream goes particularly well with hot fruit pies, the contrast in temperature adding greatly to the enjoyment.

Ingredients
Pastry
3 cups all-purpose flour
½ cup butter, cut into small pieces
2 oz ground almonds
2 tablespoons superfine sugar

Filling
1½ lb blueberries
¼ teaspoon ground cinnamon
8 tablespoons superfine sugar
2 tablespoons arrowroot

Directions
1. Sift the flour into a mixing bowl and add the butter. Rub together gently with your fingertips until the mixture resembles fine breadcrumbs. Stir in the ground almonds and sugar and enough cold water to form a soft dough.

2. Preheat the oven to 400°F. On a lightly floured surface, roll the pastry out and line a deep 8-inch pie pan. Cover the pastry shell with a piece of baking parchment and heap baking beans on top.

3. Use the remaining pastry to make thick strips for the lattice top.

4. Cook the pastry shell for 10 minutes or until the pastry is slightly golden, crisply and cooked through.

5. Place the blueberries and cinnamon in a pan with the superfine sugar and simmer very gently until tender and the juice begins to flow.

6. Blend the arrowroot with a little water to form a smooth paste and mix it into the blueberries. Stir carefully over a gentle heat until the juice thickens to a syrupy consistency.

7. Spoon the fruit into the pastry shell, arrange the strips on top to form a lattice. The return to the oven for another 10 mins or until the pastry is golden.

8. Dust with icing sugar, serve hot or cold with cream or ice cream.

Makes 6-8 servings.

CHOCOLATE FUDGE BROWNIES

America invented brownies and now everyone loves them, which is not surprising once you've tasted them. Serve them warm.

Ingredients

¾ cup soft margarine
¼ cup hazelnuts, chopped
Scant cup dark brown sugar
2 eggs, beaten
1–2 tablespoons corn or maple
 syrup
2 tablespoons cocoa powder, sifted
Scant cup wholegrain flour
2 teaspoons ground ginger

Topping

5 oz dark chocolate, broken into
 pieces
6 tablespoons light brown sugar
4 tablespoons margarine
⅔ cup heavy cream

Directions

1. Preheat the oven to 350°F. Grease and line a deep 7-inch-square cake pan.

2. Cream together the margarine and sugar until fluffy. Add the eggs, syrup and the dry ingredients, then blend together until smooth. Spoon the mixture into the pan and level the top.

Bake for 35–40 minutes or until firm. Leave to cool in the pan.

3. Melt the chocolate, sugar and margarine for the topping together, stir in the cream, then cook gently for 1–2 minutes, stirring constantly.

4. Cut the warm brownies into squares and pour on the chocolate sauce.

5. To serve cold, leave the brownies in the pan and allow both brownies and sauce to cool, then spread or swirl the sauce over the top of the brownies. Cut into squares.

Makes 16 squares.

ANGEL FOOD CAKE

This American classic is a dieter's dream – no fat, no cholesterol, and not too many calories! And it is not difficult to make. Although little is known of its origins, the cake has been popular thoughout America since the late-nineteenth century.

Ingredients:
5 tablespoons flour, sifted
1 tablespoon cornstarch
Generous cup superfine sugar
10 large egg whites
1 teaspoon cream of tartar
1½ teaspoons vanilla extract.

Decoration:
Decorate with fresh fruit, mint leaves and whipped cream.

Preparation:
1. Preheat the oven to 350°F. Sift the flour, cornstarch and 1/4 cup of sugar into a large bowl. Do this three times to incorporate as much air as possible.

2. Using an electric whisk, beat the egg whites with the cream of tartar in a large, perfectly clean bowl until stiff. Gradually whisk in the rest of the sugar, a little at a time, until the mixture becomes thick and glossy.

3. Gently fold in the flour mixture and vanilla extract until evenly blended, then transfer to a 10-inch ring mold (do not grease). Bake for 35–40 minutes until well risen and golden on top. Turn the cake out onto a wire rack and leave to cool.

4. Transfer the cake to a serving dish. Decorate as you like and serve. The cake will store well in an airtight tin.

Makess 18–20 servings

S'MORES

These classic campfire treats will take you back to your younger days. You don't need a campfire to make them, though. You can roast the marshmallows on wooden sticks over any open flame: a fire in the fireplace or a barbecue grill.

Ingredients
4 large graham crackers
2 bars of chocolate
4–8 marshmallows

Directions
1. Break the graham crackers in half so that there is a top and bottom for each s'more. Break the bars of chocolate in half and lay each piece on a graham cracker half.

2. Put the marshmallows on the ends of wooden sticks, using 1–2 per person. (Don't use unbent coat hangers; the metal gets hot.) Roast the marshmallows over

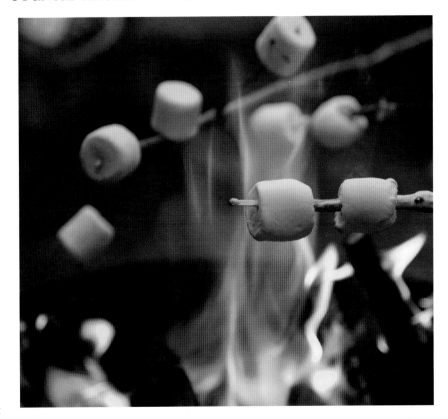

an open flame until they are done to your liking. (Some like to roast them slowly.

Some like to stick them directly in the flame so that the outside is burnt and the inside melted.)

3. Place the marshmallow on its stick between the top and bottom graham crackers and the chocolate. Hold onto the graham crackers and pull the stick out to avoid touching the hot marshmallows and burning your fingers.

Makes 4 servings.

HONEY, PECAN & RYE CAKE

This moist cake is full of nutty flavor. It is a delicious end to a meal, or as a cake to eat with coffee.

Ingredients

1 cup all-purpose flour
1 cup medium rye flour
¼ cup chopped pecans
¼ cup pecans, left whole
⅔ cup honey
⅔ cup granulated sugar
¼ cup canola oil
2 large eggs
2 teaspoons baking soda
1 teaspoon ground cinnamon
½ teaspoon ground nutmeg
¼ teaspoon ground ginger
½ teaspoon salt
¼ cup water

Directions

1 Preheat the oven to 275°F. Grease and flour a medium-sized bread pan.

2 With an electric mixer set on a low speed (or mix by hand), thoroughly combine all the ingredients, retaining some of the chopped and whole pecan nuts for the final decoration.

3 Pour the mixture into the pan and bake for about 75 minutes or until a skewer, when inserted into the cake, comes out clean.

4 Leave to cool completely in the pan, then turn out and decorate the top of the cake with the reserved chopped and whole pecans.

Serves 6–8

STRAWBERRY SHORTCAKE

Strawberries are classic, but any soft fruits can be substituted as well as sweetened crème fraîche or a mixture of half sour cream, half regular cream.

Ingredients
1½ cups butter, softened
1 scant cup superfine sugar
2⅓ cups flour, sifted
1 cup cornstarch, sifted
8 oz strawberries, hulled and
 wiped
1¼ cups whipped cream

Directions
1. Work the butter, sugar, flour and cornstarch gently together using your fingertips, then turn onto a floured surface and knead the pastry briefly until smooth.

2. Roll out the pastry to approx ½ inch thick. Make 12 rounds using a cutter if possible. Lay on cookie sheets and chill for 10 minutes. Preheat the oven to 325°F.

3. Bake the pastry circles for 15-20 minutes. When firm but not browned, remove from the oven.

4. Halve the strawberries. Take a shortcake round and pipe a dollop of cream, then add a layer of strawberries then another dollop of cream then add another top as a round.

5. Garnish with more cream and a strawberry on each shortcake.

Makes 6 servings.

INDEX